With contributions from:
D. E. B. Bates
J. R. Haynes
W. R. Fitches
D. K. Loydell
A. Cullum
R. Cave
A. P. Jones
W. T. Pratt
J. R. Davies
R. A. Waters
D. Wilson

Edited by
J. T. Greensmith

Dedication

For 30 years Alan Wood was Professor of Geology and Head of the Department at Aberystwyth. During that time he took a keen interest in both the geology and geomorphology of mid-Wales; indeed, it was his initiative that lead to the drilling of the Mochras Borehole in 1967 that triggered the subsequent geological exploration of Cardigan Bay and St. George's Channel.

His enthusiasm for teaching geology to the younger generation and particularly his love of the 'Aber Grits' caused him to initiate a guide for the Aberystwyth District, but ill health prevented realization of the project. This volume is dedicated to his memory.

ISBN 0-900717-77-7

The Aberystwyth District

CONTENTS

The Aberystwyth District

LIST OF FIGURES

contd.

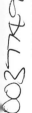

LIST OF FIGURES (continued)

The Aberystwyth District

PREFACE

The area around the University town of Aberystwyth has been recognised as possessing fascinating geology for over 100 years. It is the cradle of Welsh Basin studies not least because of the quality of exposure along the Cardigan Bay coast and the importance of the fossiliferous sites near Plynlimon. In addition to this Lower Palaeozoic geology, the area is known for the variety of its geomorphology, particularly glacial landforms, and modern sedimentary environments. This guide aims to offer the user itineraries that contain as much of this rich variety as possible, although there is an emphasis, in the first eight itineraries, on the Aberystwyth Grits and Borth Mudstones formations so clearly exposed along the coast. Where appropriate, the itinerary descriptions incorporate all the most recent ideas on the area, but to assist those with limited specialist knowledge appendices and a glossary are included.

Maps

Topographical: 1:50,000 Sheet 135 Aberystwyth, Sheet 145 Cardigan, Sheet 146 Lampeter and Llandovery, Sheet 124 Dolgellau and Sheet 125 Bala & Lake Vyrnwy.
Topographical: 1:25,000 Sheets for the Ponterwyd area are SN78, SN77 and SN87.

Geological: 1:100,000 Central Wales Mining Field
1: 50,000 Sheet 163 Aberystwyth (Solid and Drift)
1:50,000 Sheet 178 Llanilar (Solid and Drift)
New 1:250,000 bilingual map of Wales produced by the British Geological Survey.

The Aberystwyth District

Itineraries in relation to the local stratigraphy

Period	Epoch	Itinerary
	Holocene	
Quaternary	Pleistocene	9 to 12
Silurian	Llandovery	1 to 8 and 15c to 19
	Ashgill	15a and 15b
	Caradoc	13
Ordovician	Llandeilo	
	Llanvirn	
	Arenig	12
	Tremadoc	
Cambrian	Merioneth	14
	St David's	

Lithostratigraphic and biostratigraphic details are to be found in Appendix 1 and, where relevant, in the several sectional introductions.

THE ABERYSTWYTH GRITS AND BORTH MUDSTONES FORMATIONS (M.R.D., D.K.L., W.R.F. & D.E.B.B.)

The Aberystwyth Grits Formation and the Borth Mudstones Formation (Llandovery) are magnificently displayed in the cliffs of the Cardigan Bay coast, and minute details of sedimentation can be observed on the polished rock surfaces of the intertidal zone. The series of coastal exposures from New Quay to Borth shows a fine longitudinal section through these Silurian sedimentary rocks which have been interpreted as turbidity current deposits. A proximal, or near to source, facies is seen at New Quay while the deposits in the north show distal characters including fineness of grain and lateral persistence of even, thin beds indicating deposition further from the source area. Strata north of Harp Rock (Wallog) belong to the Borth Mudstones Formation; these are the distal equivalents of the earliest sediments of the Aberystwyth Grits Formation exposed at New Quay and Cei Bach. Correlation between the northern and southern sections has been made possible through the use of graptolites (for details of the lithostratigraphy and biostratigraphy see Appendix 1). Fold axes are generally parallel to the coastline, and to the northerly direction of sedimentary transport. Plunge is southwards in the

The Aberystwyth District

north of the region and northwards in the south so that the highest beds (youngest) occur towards the centre of the outcrop, around Llanrhystud (see below for further structural details).

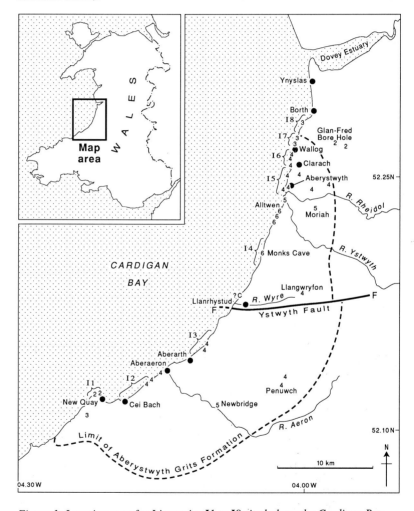

Figure 1: Location map for Itineraries I1 to I8 sited along the Cardigan Bay coast, which are principally concerned with the Aberystwyth Grits Formation and the Borth Mudstones Formation. Numbers 2 to 6 refer to graptolite subzones, and ?C refers to the crispus Biozone. The Glan-Fred Borehole penetrated the Borth Mudstones Formation Subzone 2.

The Aberystwyth District

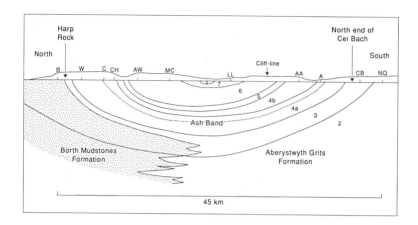

Figure 2: Schematic cross-section to show the broadly synclinal form of the coastal exposures as revealed by the biozonal evidence. The two formations are drawn in simplified form to show the relationship between biostratigraphy and lithostratigraphy. NQ = New Quay, CB = Cei Bach, A = Aberaeron, AA = Aberarth, LL = Llanrhystud, MC = Monk's Cave, AW = Allt Wen, CH = Constitution Hill, C = Clarach, W = Wallog and B = Borth.

The whole sequence may be viewed as a partially preserved, small, deep water (500m) submarine fan characterised by sediment deposition from turbid flows. Turbid flows are usually associated with the transfer of sediment from shallow water, nearshore sites to deep water where the deposited material forms a fan-shaped body. Failure of a body of sediment lying on a slope can result in a downslope density flow. Debris flows are density flows consisting of an unsorted mixture of coarse and fine material that can translate down slope into turbid flows. These turbid flows consist of a grain suspension that, with slope energy, rapidly becomes turbulent and self sustaining. An excess of density of the grain suspension over the surrounding sea water plus the slope factor induces and then ensures flow. Turbulence maintains the grains in suspension. These flows are termed turbidity currents. As the slope energy decreases the larger and denser grains collect at the base of the flow to form a traction carpet. This rapidly moving grain carpet can be strongly erosive, fluting and grooving the sea floor. The grain distribution within the carpet is usually graded. Both types of erosive structures are common in the Aberystwyth Grits Formation. Progressive sedimentation then occurs, with associated depositional bedforms including plane parallel bedding, ripple cross-lamination and convolute bedding. Ripple migration in an environment where grains are settling from suspension generates climbing ripples, whilst convolution is due to bed shear.

The Aberystwyth District

On the upper fan density flows are invariably confined to channels with banks or levees. Towards the bottom of the slope the channels broaden, thus encouraging flow dispersal that causes loss of carrying capacity and encourages sedimentation in the form of fan lobes. Density flows are also diluted through mixing with the surrounding sea water and flow stripping, both of which cause loss of carrying ability and progressive sedimentation. Sedimentation occurs as a series of fining-upward sequences identified as Tabcde, the Bouma cycle.

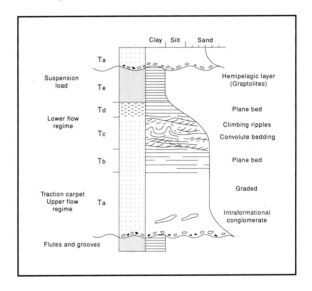

Figure 3: Graphic log of the full Bouma cycle Tabcde with sand, silt and clay lithologies in the left hand column and grain sizes with erosional and depositional structures on the right. Although dominantly fining-upward, reversed grading, or coarsening-upward, can occur in the lower part of the cycle. Whilst Ta and Tb reflect high transport velocities or upper flow regime conditions, a layer of fast moving grains (traction carpet) may form at or close to the bed. Lower flow regime refers to slower transporting flow conditions and the formation of ripples at the sediment-water interface. Redrawn and modified from Ancient Sedimentary Environments by R.C. Selley. Reproduced here with permission from Chapman & Hall.

The locations of the various itineraries and the graptolite subzones of the Aberystwyth Grits Formation and Borth Mudstones Formation and their stratigraphical relationships are shown in Figures 1 and 2. For details of the Bouma turbidite cycle notation see Figure 3.

The Aberystwyth District

STRUCTURES OF THE COASTAL ZONE

The west-central area of Wales developed as a marginal basin, located on the southern flank of an ocean, in the period from the Late Precambrian to the Early Palaeozoic. Sedimentary and volcanic fill, which ranges from Precambrian to Silurian in age, occurred during an extensional phase that was succeeded by a compressional episode in response to plate collision processes, mainly in the Early Devonian. Horizontal shortening produced folds with wavelengths of 1 to 5 kilometres and amplitudes of 1 to 2 kilometres. These structures are usually periclinal and thus create ovoid patterns of rock outcrop. Smaller-scale folds with wavelengths of 200 to 1500 m are well seen in the coastal cliffs as are folds of smaller scale with 10 m amplitudes. Fold axes are generally parallel to the coast, approximately NNE-SSW.

Cleavage is common in the mudstones, with 5mm spacing, but is more widely spaced and poorly defined in siltstones and sandstones. Although frequently axial-planar or with a fanning relationship with most folds, it can be seen to transect folds. This feature of transection of folds by sinistral cleavage is a consequence of transpressional deformation produced by oblique plate collision.

Faults have a Caledonoid or NE-SW or nearly N-S strike direction. Some of these faults are end-Caledonian in age with a strike-slip sense of movement. Much of central Wales is cut by ENE faults that displace the earlier folds and other faults. These later dip slip faults are frequently mineralised and are probably Early Variscan in age. Bedding planes, where they act as detachment surfaces, are commonly marked by quartz veining.

GEOMORPHOLOGY AND GLACIAL DEPOSITS

Geomorphologically, the coastline is interesting. Over the last 6,000 years, sections of solid rock cliffs have been exhumed from behind glacial deposits, and thus these cliffs predate the last part of the Pleistocene period (they are pre-Devensian in age). The grass-covered 'coastal bevel' that forms so prominent a feature above the seemingly modern cliffs is believed to have been cut, at least in part, by meltwater streams when ice abutted the coast. Two main boulder clays or tills occur, a Welsh Till, grey-blue in colour with local erratics, and an Irish Sea Till, light red in colour, calcareous, and containing far-travelled boulders. The last glacial event was a period of permafrosting of previous deposits and intense solifluction. For details of the Quaternary sequences please refer to Appendix 2. Rising sea-level, particularly over the last 8,000 years, has reworked the till deposits, created coastal sand spits, influenced the development of estuaries and eroded the cliffs carved from solid rock. Based on the width of the marine platform the rate of erosion of the solid rock cliffs probably exceeds 5 mm per year; the till cliffs are receding at a much faster rate.

The Aberystwyth District

THE FOSSILS OF THE AREA

With the exception of a few bivalves from the Rheidol Gorge, and a handful of brachiopods collected from the Aberystwyth Grits Formation between Aberystwyth and Clarach, the body fossils of western mid-Wales are exclusively pelagic organisms. Orthoconic (i.e. straight, conical) nautiloids, ancestors of the modern *Nautilus*, occur sporadically at several inland localities (particularly in the *triangulatus* Biozone, Middle Llandovery of the Rheidol Gorge), but are rare within the Aberystwyth Grits Formation, although bounce marks made by orthoconic nautiloid shells, that were carried within turbidity currents, have been reported from the bases of sandstones from many localities within the formation's outcrop area. By far the most common body fossils in the Llandovery of western mid-Wales are, however, the remains of graptolites. Graptolites were planktonic, colonial organisms which swarmed in the Silurian seas. They almost became extinct during the end-Ordovician glaciation, but recovered in the Llandovery, attaining a diversity maximum during the early part of the Middle Llandovery (*triangulatus* Biozone). The rapid evolution, particularly of monograptaceans (graptolites with a single row of thecae - these were tubes which housed the individual zooids of the colony), has enabled palaeontologists to erect a very detailed biostratigraphy for the Llandovery, individual subzones having a duration of as little as 100,000-200,000 years.

Finding graptolites within the Rheidol Gorge should not pose any problems. Any dark, laminated mudstone should contain them. Avoid bioturbated horizons, as the graptolites within these have largely been destroyed by burrowing activity. The graptolites in the Rheidol Gorge are famous world-wide for their exquisite preservation as pyrite internal moulds, formed as a result of the reaction of hydrogen sulphide (produced by anaerobic decay of the graptolites soft tissues) with iron within the sediment.

The graptolites of the Aberystwyth Grits Formation are much less easy to find, unless you know where to look! Sometimes graptolites may be found within turbidite sandstones. They tend to be aligned (in the direction of turbidity current flow) and current-sorted such that one species may dominate the fauna of any one sandstone at a particular locality. A more profitable approach to graptolite-hunting is to look at the deposits formed between turbidity incursions into the area. These are preserved only at certain localities, these being places where trace fossils are absent (the trace fossils indicate that the bottom waters of the Welsh Basin at the time of deposition of the turbidite were oxygenated - any graptolites falling to the sea bed at such times would have been destroyed by the activities of the benthos or would have decayed leaving no trace in the rock record). Good localities for collecting graptolites from the Aberystwyth Grits Formation and examining the deposits in which they are preserved are **Loc.1** Itinerary 6 (N of Clarach) and immediately south of Harp Rock (Itinerary 7). Graptolites from these localities have been found with a length of more that 1 m (but a width of only 0.5-2 mm!). To find them look in the dark mudstone horizons (often only 1 mm or less thick) between turbidites. Sometimes these mudstones are plastered to the overlying turbidite sandstone. More commonly the rock has split along the graptolite horizon and it is possible to crawl over the former sea floor in search of the fossils (a hand lens is useful for appreciating them fully). Unfortunately, at some levels, because the graptolitic horizon has formed a line of weakness, bedding-plane slip has occurred along the mudstone and any graptolite remains have been obliterated by slickensliding.

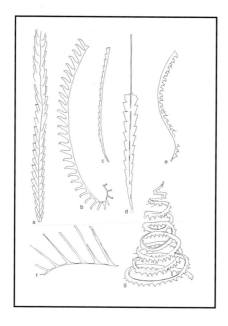

Figure 4: Some common graptolites found in mid-Wales.
  (a) Normalograptus persculptus. (b) Demirastrites triangulatus.
  (c) Pristiograptus renaudi. (d) Parakidograptus acuminatus.
  (e) Stimulograptus utilis. (f) Rastrites linnaei.
  (g) Spirograptus guerichi. All are x 1.5.

A small selection of graptolites from western mid-Wales is illustrated in Figure 4. Please bear in mind that there are several hundred different species known from the area. Those interested in identifying their finds should consult the relevant Palaeontographical Society Monographs.

The Aberystwyth District

Ichnofauna

The Aberystwyth Grits Formation is rich in trace fossil assemblages and attempts have been made to link them to specific facies. *Helminthoida crassa* commonly occurs on the flute-cast bases of sandstones which are thicker than the underlying mudstones, and *Squadmodictyon, Megagrapton* and *Helminthopsis* where the sandstone and mudstone thicknesses are approximately equal. *Palaeodictyon* occurs on the base of sandstones which are thinner than the underlying mudstones. It appears, therefore, that the trace fossil assemblages preserved are mainly controlled by the erosive power of the succeeding turbidite, and that, given an oxic sea floor, all the trace fossil markers were present. When the trace fossils are plotted against the graptolite subzones, there is no obvious correlation between time and assemblage; nor is there an obvious correlation between trace fossils and facies types. Note that the trace fossil assemblages are highly characteristic of deep water deposits - similar assemblages are found in such environments throughout the geological record.

Complex feeding traces (including regularly meandering and spiral patterns) reflect the activity of the marker. In a deep-water environment, where currently activity is generally low (remember that turbidity currents only entered the Welsh Basin infrequently, probably at intervals of approximately a hundred to a thousand years) most edible organic matter has settled out from suspension and is incorporated within the sediment. The most appropriate feeding strategy is to ingest the sediment, extracting organic nourishment and void the residue. This is known as deposit feeding. Look closely at any of the feeding traces - note that the organism seemed able to avoid any area of sediment that had already been processed (and would thus have been barren of edible organic matter). Today, this is achieved by the organism leaving a trail of slime that can then be sensed chemically - it seems that Silurian 'worms' and molluscs behaved in a very similar way.

WARNING The tidal range at Aberystwyth is considerable and many sections are inaccessible during the whole neap tide period. Spring tides occur around the time of the full moon and a fortnight later and for about 6 days the sections are then accessible in the afternoon and early evening. Extreme low tide is about 7 hours after full tide; care should be taken on a rising tide since many of the cliffs are unscaleable. Periglacial deposits at the top of the cliffs are an especial hazard to the climber. Tide tables are available from the Aberystwyth harbour office, newsagents and bookshops in the area and should be consulted.

The Aberystwyth District

ITINERARIES

1. NEW QUAY, SN 38686044. Character of earliest AGF proximal
turbidites, amalgamated beds, sedimentary dykes and sills. Figures 5 and 6
(M.R.D., D.K.L. & A.C.)

Drive S from Aberystwyth along the A487 as far as Llanarth where you turn
right to New Quay. In New Quay take the road that descends to the harbour
(note a one way system operates), swing left past the end of the pier and take
the first right. Proceed along a narrow promenade, leaving your vehicle in the
car park on the left hand side and walk to the turning point at the road end,
close to a fish processing factory. The 30 m thick succession in New Quay
Head Old Quarry (**Loc. 1**) consists of beds that thicken upward for 6 m to be
replaced by a succession (>8 m) of thinner strata. 70 cm thick sandstones are
separated by about 2 cm of mudstones and siltstones. These thick (Tabe)
sequences, with the sandstones frequently occurring as amalgamated beds, up
to 2 m thick with water escape structures, are suggestive of episodes of high
frequency turbidity current influxes. The New Quay rocks represent the oldest
dated sequence (Subzone 2) in the AGF: although absent over the rest of the
coastal outcrop, rocks of this age have been recovered from the Glan-fred
borehole which penetrated the Borth Mudstones Formation (Figures 1 and 2).

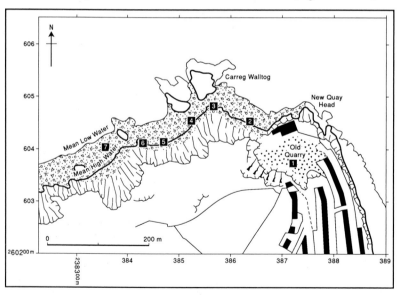

*Figure 5: Location map for Itinerary 1, New Quay area. Numbers refer to
localities mentioned in the text; solid black rectangles are buildings.
Symbol with small circles refers to pebble and cobble beach.*

The Aberystwyth District

Access to the beach is by climbing down the steep dip slope of an anticline that lies immediately west of the factory (probably not suitable for the elderly and the very young). Care is required as shell waste frequently covers the rock surface. The beds on the left (**Loc. 2**) are folded into a series of faulted anticlines and synclines. Examine the beds dipping uniformly north of west, the bases of which are polished by pebble scour. The beds show differences from those seen at Aberystwyth (Itinerary 5). This is attributed to them being nearer the source area; they do of course also belong to an older graptolite subzone. Note that amalgamated beds are common, frequently with reversed grading; that is the upper part is coarser and may be load-casted down into the lower fine grained part. Other greywackes are unusually coarse (up to granule grade) for this basin of deposition and the grain texture is nearly uniform. The thin bedded mudstones between show large numbers of fine laminations. At least three cycles of thick-bedded, coarse grained units succeeded by thin-bedded, fine grained turbidite units may be observed.

Pass between a large sea stack called Carreg Walltog and the cliff face, and turn left as soon as a pebble band appears again. Note that the cliff or steep rock face on the left, consists of a thick amalgamated bed involving at least 4 episodes of input, each up to granule grade. Immediately on the left, in a mudstone below an amalgamated greywacke, is a sedimentary sill (**Loc. 3**). An amalgamated greywacke bed at beach level appears to be the source of the sill. The point of origin of the sill is affected by cleavage, concentrated here because of the differing competency of the beds. Trace the sill along. About one metre above beach level tiny sedimentary dykes rise into the bed above. They are approximately parallel to the strike of the beds. Each runs into a joint in the greywacke above, and their presence may have determined the position of these joints. The thin dykes are minutely folded by compaction of the mudstone around a thicker dyke which has been expanded to a barrel shape and causes the sill below to bulge downwards. The sill finally thins out about 4 metres above beach level. Note that many of the coarse-grained amalgamated beds load down into the underlying mudstones.

Walk a few metres further away from the sea, keeping close to the cliff face. Observe a 3 metre thick finely bedded facies (**Loc. 4**). Most of the individual beds are laminated and show foreset bedding. The facies consists of (Tcde) thinly bedded turbidities in which sandy basal beds, showing well developed ripple cross-lamination and lee side preservation only, are capped by silt and mud drapes. These formed from turbidity currents of intermediate density. The log (Figure 6) is located at this site and shows the principal thick-bedded facies and a finer series.

The Aberystwyth District

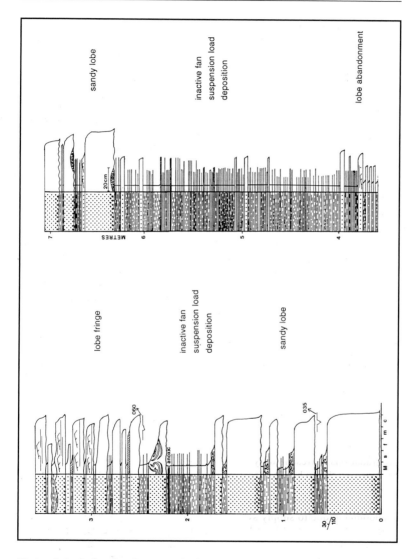

Figure 6: Log of rock sequence at locality 4, Itinerary 1, see Figure 44 for symbol explanation. The interpretations are for guidance.

Pass around a rippled dip slope, the upper surface of a massive greywacke, and observe various sedimentary features of beds below, Well developed load casts can be seen, and more slumped beds occur, their matrix being muddier than the normal greywackes. Continue south-westwards for about 20 metres from the nearly vertical face in which the slumped beds occur. Large subangular blocks appear in the beach, and in the cliff face (facing the sea and nearly at right angles to the last mentioned exposure) a thick mudstone can be seen a metre or so above beach level. This mudstone thins rapidly southwestwards, and observation shows that it occupies a curved hollow in a thick greywacke (**Loc. 5**). This is interpreted as a slide-scar on the sea floor, later almost entirely filled by mud. It will be seen that the greywacke immediately above the thick lens of mud, which there is about 30 cm thick, itself thins southwards to a few centimetres. Possibly this thickening is due to compaction of the freshly deposited mud by the weight of the sediment as the greywacke itself was deposited.

Look southwestwards, along the beach. A jagged promontory (**Loc. 6**) shows beds dipping seawards. Pass through a narrow cleft between this promontory and the main cliff. A plunging anticline with a faulted axial zone is seen to the left. A massive bed (**Loc. 7**) is at beach level in the left limb and upward projections extend into the rather thick mudstone above. The thinner projections are contorted, the thicker expanded, presumably by compaction of the mudstone. These features are interpreted as sedimentary dykes, injected upwards, with water escape structures, and suggestive of episodes of high frequency turbidity current influxes. They are well seen again, above the same bed, on the right-hand side of the fold where the mudstone with dykes forms a prominent steeply seaward dipping bedding plane. Beyond this point sole markings (groove casts and flute casts) confirm that the transporting current was from the southwest towards the northeast, and some good sections of load casts can be seen on the upper surface of beds.

Employing the principle that facies lying on top of one another were formed beside each other in space (Walther's Law), the pattern of sedimentation at New Quay may be envisaged as repeated lobe progradations represented by the thickening-upward cycles, invariably followed by thinly bedded facies seen as deposition on the fringes of lobes or between lobes. Very thinly bedded sequences, such as those shown on the log between 4 and 6 metres, probably represent episodes of abandonment due to supply switching. Sediment supply during periods of lobe progradation must have been rich and rapid, thus encouraging the formation of water escape structures, soft-sediment loading and amalgamated beds. Re-examine the exposure and the log and see whether you reach similar conclusions. For example, it might be argued that the thin bedded sequences reflect small scale slope apron failure at times when the main supply channel was inactive.

It is possible to climb the grassy slopes and return to New Quay well above beach level.

The Aberystwyth District

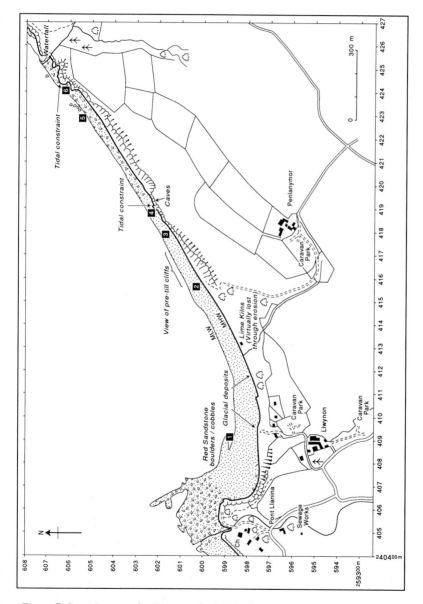

Figure 7: Location map for Itinerary 2, Cei Bach section.

The Aberystwyth District

2. CEI BACH TO GILFACH, SN 415600. Coastal geomorphology, amalgamated beds, washouts and sole markings. Figures 7 and 8. (The distance from the start to the waterfall is 2 km, and from the waterfall to Gilfach 1 km. The itinerary may be split into two trips for convenience.) (M.R.D., D.K.L. & A.C.).

Proceeding southwards from Aberaeron towards Cardigan turn right at the cross-roads just past the milestone reading 'Cardigan 19 miles'. Continue westwards towards the sea to the end of the road. Take the steps to the beach. Parking can be difficult, particularly at weekends.

Turn right and walk northeastwards along the beach. The gravel spread on the beach (**Loc.1**) contains numerous cobbles of red sandstone of a Triassic aspect. These may have been trawled from the floor of Cardigan Bay by Irish Sea Ice (see Figures 45 and 48). When about 400 m from the first solid rock cliffs observe how the cliff face is covered by scrub vegetation and runs obliquely southwards behind the till (**Loc. 2**). The cliff face here was cut to nearly its present form before the till was deposited. In fact, the whole coastline as far as New Quay consists of glacial till that was trapped in the lee of New Quay Head. Parts of the pre-till cliff line lie up to a kilometre inland. Above the cliffs the coastal bevel can be seen, and appears to steepen seawards, above the cliffs in the distance near Gilfach. At this locality, a rocky beach platform is absent. Along this coast, when a rocky beach platform is absent the cliffs are of interglacial age, as here and north of Monk's Cave. The beach platform near Gilfach proves that those cliffs were cut when the sea was at its present level.

Exposed in 35 m high cliffs 600 m NE of the lime kilns, is a nearly horizontal sequence of the AGF of Subzone 3 age, with little evidence for tectonic activity except for small listric faults (note that the beds N of Wallog and the highest part of the Borth Mudstones Formation are also of Subzone 3 age). The sequence (**Loc. 3 to 4**) consists of plane-parallel Tcde turbidite units about 15 cm thick near the base of the cliff. Here, cross-lamination displays ripples of wavelengths over 15 cm and up to 50 cm. Clusters of turbidite units coarsen and thicken upward, such that many consist of the sequence (Tabcde), occasionally with groove casts orientated east-northeast. The thicker greywackes often contain mudstone fragments seen as intraformational conglomerates. Above, they thin upward progressively with variation in unit thicknesses. Amalgamated beds reflect premature re-introduction of coarser sediment with attendant density inversion and 'loading'. These beds provide strong evidence of a rapid repetition of events. In addition, 8 or 10 Tde units occur in packets up to 50 cm thick. Several horizons reveal soft sediment deformation in which there is slumped bedding with turnovers in excess of 1 m. The broad orientation of the slumping direction is north. Thus, throughout this section bedding is thinner and grain size finer than in the underlying Subzone 2 seen at New Quay. The turbidite sequence, seen at the first appearance of the

The Aberystwyth District

cliffs (**Loc. 3**) from behind the glacial deposits to within 100 m of the prominent headland at **Loc. 6**, may be interpreted as representing a distal-lobe environment with incursions of sandy-lobe turbidites about 16 units thick which decline upwards. The whole sequence may be viewed as a prograding phase followed by retrograding or a gradual decline in sediment supply.

A short distance north (higher in the succession) the thick mudstone beds cease and are replaced by greywacke-dominated beds of Subzone 4a. Just below these beds, at an indentation in the cliff, mudstone bands carry darker mudstone fragments, and some are directly overlain by thin, lighter greywackes, conspicuously load-casted down into them. The sudden incursion of coarse-grained turbidites close to the Subzone 3/4a boundary coincides closely in time with that observed at Harp Rock (see Itinerary 7), and may well indicate a fan-wide event.

Beyond a small cave thick mudstones occur again, and a slumped bed occurs with well developed load casts above. The associated mudstones are obviously formed of bands of slightly differing grain size, each probably having been deposited by a separate turbidity current. At the corner, where the cliff-line turns eastwards, again a turbidity current load appears to have been 'frozen' in the act of eroding an earlier deposited greywacke. The lower part of the amalgamated bed consists of a large number of rolls of greywacke, at right angles to the current direction, each with its upper side inverted. This unusual bed is the sixth below the thickest (45 cm) bed of this part of the section. From here on the cliff is partly grass-covered and lies behind a storm beach, but it is instructive to examine the cliff (**Loc. 5**) where faults and minor associated folds occur. Wave-washed sections are not seen until the northern headland is reached (**Loc. 6**).

At the northern end of the beach note the virtual absence of mudstones between greywackes in the cliff. Signs of current action and convolute bedding are common. Sole marks are poorly developed. Beyond the thrust fault, mudstones are seen at beach level with thin turbidite bands. The latter differ from those at Aberystwyth in showing foreset bedding and other signs of more rapid current flow.

Walk around the next headland (only possible at low spring tides) noting the large (present day) worm colonies on the rocks. The first good exposures are in a bay with a waterfall (SN 4255 6070) at the head (**Loc. 7**). The north cliff face shows well polished surfaces on which the signs of current action in the thinner greywackes can be clearly seen. Some of the thicker beds can be seen to split; one in particular passes from a single to a double to a triple bed as it is followed seawards. Such an occurrence is interpreted as being due to downcutting by the current that deposited the topmost part. The current eroded away the middle and then the basal greywacke, leaving only one bed in their place. Proceed round the seaward end of this cliff, preferably on a falling tide,

The Aberystwyth District

and the three beds just mentioned can be seen clearly to be separated by mudstones at beach level, and thus were deposited successively, but after considerable intervals of time.

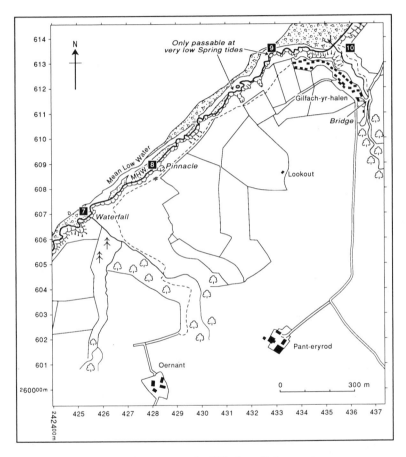

Figure 8: Location map for Itinerary 2, Gilfach-yr-Halen section.

Continue across a small bay with a pebble beach, pass around a headland, in front of which is a bare rock platform, and enter a much longer embayment with a well developed beach of coarse pebbles. A sea stack will be seen high up the beach, about a third of the way along. Just north of this stack thick beds are seen at or near beach level (**Loc. 8**). One of these beds can be traced for over 300 m to the northeast until it runs out to sea.

The Aberystwyth District

Pass round a sea stack at near low tide level observing that the thick-bedded greywackes gradually pass into a thin bedded series upwards. The character of the thin bedded greywackes can easily be studied at the base of the cliffs and in polished surfaces on the beach boulders. The variation of thickness and evidence of rapid current flow are strikingly different from the characters of distal beds at Aberystwyth itself.

When the glacial cliffs of Gilfach can first be seen a thin light-coloured volcanic ash band can be observed in the thin-bedded series about halfway up the cliffs on the right. It is very similar in appearance to the ash band at Clarach (**Loc. 9**).

Walk up the path, passing cliffs formed of 18 m of gravels (**Loc. 10**) that accumulated in a meltwater channel (see diagrams 3 and 4 in Figure 47), to the bridge and then along the small road to the main A487, a distance of 2 km. It is possible to examine this part of the coastline in two stages, the first as above, as far as the northern end of Cei Bach beach, the second from Gilfach southwards to the waterfall. To reach the beach at Gilfach turn off the A487 to Gilfach-yr-Halen, do not enter the holiday centre, but turn sharply right across the bridge and park at the top of the path to the beach. Parking is difficult in summer.

3. ABERARTH TO MORFA, SN 480642. Coastal geomorphology, slumped bedding, load-casting, lobe progradation and sole markings. Figures 9, 10 and 11. (M.R.D., D.K.L. & .A.C.)

Between Aberarth and the farm called Morfa, 3 km to the north, bold cliffs occur, while both to the south and to north of this stretch of cliffs a low level plain of varied glacial deposits runs gently to the sea. The coastal bevel is truncated along the coast to be visited.

Turn seaward along the road immediately to the north of the bridge at Aberarth (SN 47956378). Parking is usually possible about 100 metres down this road. Follow the path northwards to the beach. Here the cliffs (**Loc. 1**) are composed of resedimented Welsh Blue Till (10 m), with fluvio-glacial layers of sand and gravel often present. The underlying Yellow-Grey Till (3 m) may be recognised, whilst the 4 m or so of brown Head is laterally persistent at the top of the cliffs. These cliffs are susceptible to landslip and therefore potentially dangerous. The beach platform is cut in till, whilst a wave-cut notch occurs at the base of the cliff; note the artificial fish ponds recognisable at low tide and originally built by the monks of Strata Florida Abbey. The vast majority of boulders on the beach are of local Silurian greywacke.

About 500 metres to the northeast, solid rock emerges from behind the till (**Loc. 2**), and the vertical till cliffs give way to a steep glassy slope, with a veneer of till on solid rock above the Recent cliffs. The till here mantles a

The Aberystwyth District

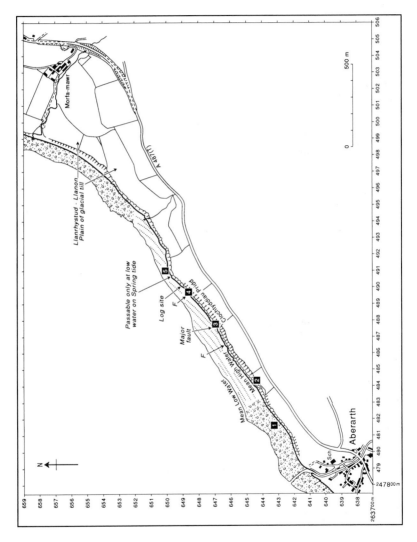

Figure 9: Location map for Itinerary 3, Aberarth to Morfa. F refers to small faults seen in the cliff face. The dotted lines on the foreshore indicate the general strike of the beds.

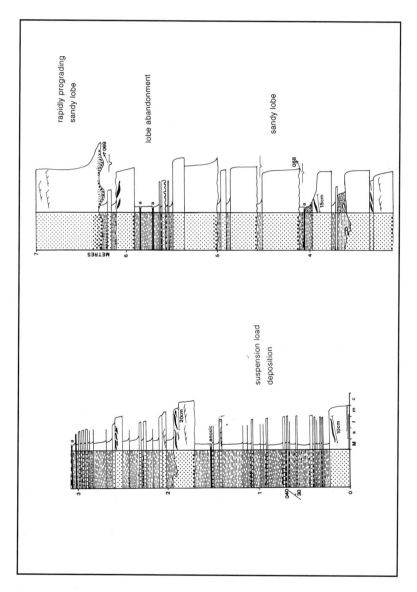

Figure 10: Log of rock sequence at locality 5, Itinerary 3, Aberarth.

The Aberystwyth District

degraded pre-till cliff. The present day rock cliff begins as a sharpening of the edge of the old cliff. As erosion becomes greater northeastwards the cut becomes more pronounced and a beach platform begins to appear, the outer margin of which is coincident with the edge of the old cliff. Walk to the edge of the sea for a panoramic view. The grassy slope vanishes northwards, as the cliffs turn landwards. Beyond this point the coastal bevel lies above high, nearly vertical cliffs, partly grass covered. The bevel can be traced southwards behind a grassy platform, above the grassy slope.

The first solid rock cliffs are formed from Aberystwyth Grits Formation turbidite beds 30-50 cm thick dipping landwards at about 40 degrees. They are of Subzone 4b age; the age also of the sequence at Craig Fawr Quarry, Penuwch (SN 589622) 10 km to the east of Aberarth. This sequence, which consists of 30 to 60 cm thick sandstone units and 8 cm thick mudstones, forms the cliffs to the northeast for more that 300 m where it is faulted against a finer sequence that persists for 120 m. This section is famous for the exceptionally complex, but clearly displayed, 'slump structures' (Figure 11). The large, elongate laminated mudstone slabs contained within a few greywackes are considered by some observers to have sunk or 'foundered'; implying a soft sediment deformation mechanism rather than being seen as intraformational 'rafts' resulting from slumping.

A small normal fault (**Loc. 3**) brings a sequence of exceptionally thick units gradually to beach level. Another fault, some 250 m along the beach (**Loc. 4**) brings massively thick sandstone units gradually to beach level. One sandstone unit consists of an amalgamated bed, 5 m thick, that persists to the small headland or promontory (**Loc. 5**). The lowest 3 m is very fine grained and thinly bedded. Above, the turbidite units both thicken and coarsen upwards, many having strongly erosive bases.

The section from **Loc. 2 to Loc. 5** displays five successive packets of strata each of a thickness of between 25 and 50 m. At the base of each packet thick, massively bedded, coarse-grained sandstones and conglomerates, with ripped-up mudstone clasts, occur. Bed thicknesses, regularly enhanced by amalgamation, gradually decline upwards within each packet. Palaeocurrent directions, indicated by the cross-bedding, range between northeastward and eastward whereas flute orientations are northeastwards. Overall, these thinning upward packets are interpreted as episodic sandy lobe progradations reflecting pulsed sediment supply.

The criteria for recognition of proximal sandy lobe sequences include a grain size range from fine conglomerate to fine sand, reverse grading or the tendency for upward coarsening of the grain sizes at the base of each bed and followed by fining upward, multiple amalgamation or sequence stacking of sandstone beds each with strongly erosive bases and evidence for downcutting. Examine the log (Figure 10) that was taken on the south side of the

The Aberystwyth District

promontory. Most of the coarse grained sandstones have deeply scoured bases with pebble and mud flake conglomerates and overlie eroded thin mudstone surfaces created by high concentration turbidity currents.

Figure 11: Photograph of the 'slumped unit' found close to the base of the cliff north of Aberarth. Note the black squares on the scale card are 1 cm.

North of the promontory where these thick beds run out to sea, a broad shallow cave is seen in which there are good examples of various casts on the undersides of the greywacke beds. An alternation of groups of thick and thin greywackes, with varying sedimentary structures, continues northwards. Examination of the thinnest beds will show them to vary in thickness and occasionally to be current bedded, both being in contrast with similar beds at Aberystwyth (Itinerary 5).

Before leaving the beach at Morfa, and walking through the farmyard buildings to return by road, look back at the cliffs, (incidentally, it is possible to return by walking along the cliff top although the path is uncertain due to persistent erosion). The coastal bevel above is prominent, with a concavity showing at its lower edge at about 70 m. Nearer to Morfa there is a sudden drop to a concavity at 30 m, the trace of a second raised platform cutting into the higher one. Below this the fossil cliff, scarcely touched by modern marine erosion, can be seen to pass behind the glacial beds of the Llanrhystud-Llanon plain.

The Aberystwyth District

4. MONK'S CAVE, SN 555745. Coastal geomorphology, glacial deposits, a packet of thick bedded sandstones and washouts. Figures 12, 13, 14, and 15. (M.R.D., D.K.L. & A.C.).

Proceed south from Aberystwyth along the A487 to just over two kilometres south of Blaenplwyf and park in a lay-by seen on the right hand side of the road (SN 564743). Here a farm track goes off to the right. Go along this track to the National Trust site called Mynachdy'r Graig and continue straight on through a gate to the right. At the first hairpin bend in the track descending the slope turn left on to a promontory (**Loc. 1**). Below is the '100 ft' platform, pinched out to the south between the bevel and the modern cliff. In this direction, also, small remnants of the '300ft' platform are visible. Continue down the track. At the point where the farm buildings are first seen (**Loc. 2**) there is a fine view both to the north and the south. The '100ft' platform itself is clearly at a lower level beyond the farm than it is on the horizon. These 'platforms', cut at slightly different levels, and all now covered by a veneer of glacial material, have united to make this fertile strip, seaward of the coastal bevel. It is probable that, whilst a '100 ft' marine platform and indeed a '300 ft' marine platform can be recognised, meltwater channels may have occupied the features; certainly the lower of the two platforms is noticeably concave in section (see Appendix 2 for further details). To the north the coastal bevel is clearly seen. Just before the last headland it descends nearly to sea-level and is unusually steep. The coastal bevel is considered to have been cut at various times; the portion behind the platforms must be of earlier date than the platforms themselves, but this part of the bevel extends below the level of the grassy platform below the observer and therefore must postdate it.

Descend the cliff face on the south side of the stream near the farm. This path is steep and slippery and should not be attempted in wet weather; this is where the ascent will be made also. To the north the 'fossil' cliff runs inland behind the till cliff and large isolated blocks at the base can be seen. Well defined Welsh Blue Till, undercut at the base, occurs for more that 1 km northwards towards Morfa Bychan. The relationships between the 'fossil' cliff and the 'till' cliff can be studied in detail immediately north of the descent point. (**Loc. 3**).

From the point where the descent was made from the farm, a 7 m thick packet of massive beds of greywacke occurs (Tb), shattered and folded by tectonic activity (**Loc. 4**). Above, in the cliff is an amalgamated bed 60 cm thick with the lower 20 cm separated by a faint bedding plane. This and the massive beds are marker horizons that can be traced for two kilometres to the south across a number of important faults. There are small scale low angle thrust faults present in the cliff. Observe ripple drift bedding and current bedding in the thin beds above and below the massive ones. Sections both parallel and transverse to the current direction can readily be examined. The packet of massive beds lies abruptly on thin bedded greywackes and mudstones. On the south side of this promontory examine the well exposed fault (see Figure 13).

The Aberystwyth District

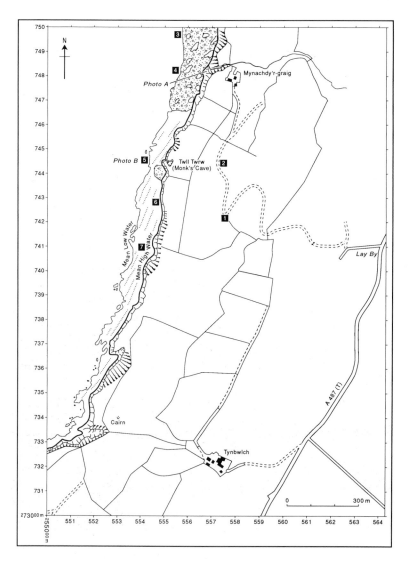

Figure 12: Location map for Itinerary 4, Monk's Cave. The dotted lines on the foreshore indicate the general strike of the beds. Photo A refers to Figure 13 and Photo B refers to Figure 14.

The Aberystwyth District

On moving southwards a slumped bed with sedimentary rolls parallel to the current direction can be seen well exposed at the base of the cliff. Two metres above it is a prominent slumped greywacke, and some two metres higher is a greywacke about 30 cm thick. The ninth bed above this shows a good washout, three beds on the landward side being replaced by a single 20 cm greywacke on the seaward face. The stages of cutting down by the current responsible for the deposition of the uppermost of the three greywackes can readily be traced. Washouts in this region are elongated in a N-S direction, indicating that they were cut by faster moving portions of the turbid current. Continue across slightly undulating beds to Monk's Cave (**Loc. 5**). This is a partly pre-till cave re-excavated, with side passages prolonged along faults (Figure 14); here the double bed is readily recognised. Passing the striking stacks in horizontal beds in which washouts can be seen, we emerge onto a wide beach (**Loc. 6**). The base of the packet of massive beds is seen in the cliffs immediately in front and in the cliffs in the far distance. At the point where the massive beds are at beach level a very fine example of slumped bedding is visible in a small cave facing south. Careful examination of the overfolded greywackes and the three thin beds above will show that they pass laterally into a thick greywacke (in fact they probably occupy a washout in it), and that folding was complete before the deposition of the three thin beds between the slumped bed and the greywacke above. Later tectonic folding, well seen on the beach platform, has affected the bed above on the same axes.

Figure 13: Photograph taken at locality 4, Itinerary 4, close to the point of descent and showing small scale faulting which brings a 7 m sequence of thick-bedded sandstones, that thin upwards, against thin-bedded turbidites.

The Aberystwyth District

Figure 14: Photograph of locality 5 Itinerary 4, showing 15 m of medium bedded turbidites each cycle consisting of Tcde and characteristic of an outer lobe environment.

Continuing southwards, thin beds below the massive beds are seen, with the sudden incoming of the massive series becoming very obvious. At the next headland and stack (**Loc. 7**) observe the height of the water and check the time carefully to avoid being cut off by the tide. Here, the slump beds are seen together with good small-scale tectonic folding and squeezing. Passing a strong tear fault, a rather rough scramble along the beach platform reveals the double and massive beds again, strikingly affected by thrusting; and in the next bay the whole succession can be seen in an impressive cliff. The slumped beds are at the base and can be studied in detail. In this extremely unfrequented spot, seals are commonly seen.

In brief, the patterns of sedimentation seen in the rocks at Monk's Cave conform to the general turbidite fan model. The rocks are of Subzone 6 age and for more that 2 km southwards there is a near continuous strike section that contains six prominent sandstone beds, frequently with disturbed or slumped beds at the top. These marker beds are underlain and overlain by thinly bedded Tcde turbidite units. That part of the section consisting of the massively bedded turbidite units (Tbcde) is persistently about 7 m thick, with large, broad flutes that display variable current directions from northwards to southeastwards. In addition, there is evidence of syn-sedimentary faulting, sand-injections and lateral facies variations. The sandstones display consistent

The Aberystwyth District

base-parallelism over a distance in excess of 2 km with no evidence of downcutting, particularly by the basal bed, whilst grain size fails to reach granule grade. The thinly bedded units, of remarkable regularity, notably at Monk's Cave, are characteristic of outer-fan to basin-plain facies, whereas the massive beds represent a sandy lobe incursion that rapidly declined, as evidenced by the thinning of the coarser grained beds, and was abandoned allowing a return to outer fan or basin plain depositional conditions (Figure 15).

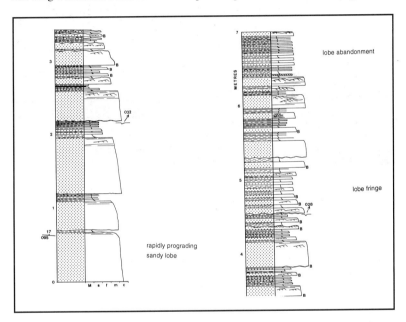

Figure 15: Log of the rocks seen at locality 4, Itinerary 4, and in the photograph Figure 13.

On the return to the point of descent examine the exposure in the light of this proposed model and judge whether it broadly explains the sequence present. A sudden introduction of coarse sediment over unconsolidated fine grained silts and muds with a high water content might explain some of the soft sediment deformation features observed (sand has a greater density than silts and clays in a water environment because of the differences in contained water).

5. ABERYSTWYTH TO CLARACH, SN 583825 to 586835. The classic section of the Aberystwyth Grits Formation: sedimentary characters of distal turbidites, sole markings and lateral correlation using sedimentary 'patterns'. Figures 16, 17, 18 and 19. (M.R.D., D.K.L., W.R.F. & A.C.).

The Aberystwyth District

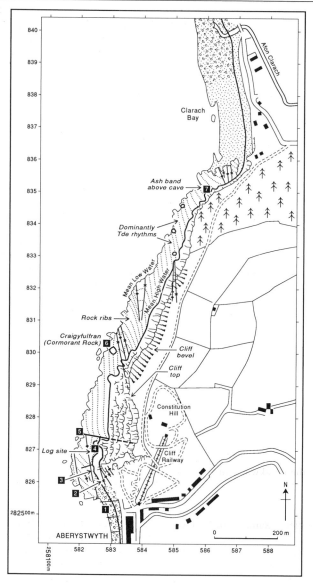

Figure 16: Location map for Itinerary 5 Aberystwyth to Clarach. Dotted lines on the foreshore indicate the general strike of the beds. A prominent concrete groyne with iron ladder can be seen on Figure 18 and is shown as a black line on the map, located between Loc. 3 and 4.

The Aberystwyth District

At the north end of the promenade at Aberystwyth (**Loc. 1**) the great majority of pebbles on the beach are of local Silurian greywacke, but among them is a considerable variety of far-travelled types, including rhyolites and porphyries from north Wales, riebeckite microgranite from Ailsa Craig and/or Mynydd Mawr, plutonic rocks and rarer jaspers and Cretaceous flints derived from the Irish Sea Till.

In the cliff (**Loc. 2**) a conspicuous anticline plunges southwards at 20 degrees, resting on a reverse fault. The fold dies out towards the north. Cleavage here and on the beach platform is stronger near the axis of the folds, but is often discordant. The beds between the fold and the breakwater are typical of the Aberystwyth Grits Formation. Greywacke bands alternate with dark shales and graded and convolute bedding can be seen. Tcde turbidite units of Subzone 4 age (Figure 1) occur at Constitution Hill (Figure 18). Individual sandstone beds are uniform in thickness and laterally extensive, showing no evidence of pinchouts or rapid thinning. Again, both sole and cross-bedding structures show directional consistency whilst convolute lamination is especially common. For details of turbidite deposition cycles please consult Appendix 1. The undersides of the beds, with flute casts and traction lineation grooves are well exposed (**Loc. 3**). The various marks indicate derivation from 20 degrees or so west of south. The thickness and spacing of greywackes are constant for a considerable distance, and enable correlation to be made across folds and faults.

The key beds in this section are the 6th, 7th and 8th of the prominent greywacke ribs counting downwards (and seawards) from the reverse fault. They are 12 cm, 19 cm and 12 cm thick, and are separated by 65 cm and 50 cm of mudstone, each with 7 light-coloured partings, the uppermost being the thickest in each case.

From the end of the breakwater observe beds dipping steeply seawards at the top of the cliffs, with nearly horizontal small scale folds. These are thrust over the landward dipping series by a reverse fault. In the first cove north of the breakwater the three key beds occur at the back of the embayment. The graphic log, Figure 17, represents part of the sequence displayed in the cove (**Loc. 4**).

Very clear examples of flute casts, bounce casts, trace fossils and current ripples transverse to the direction of transport can be seen on the underside of beds, displayed in vertical section one above the other and indicating a constant current direction. The best time to observe these features is early in the evening, when the sun shines along the bottom of the beds at a low angle. The reverse fault, associated with folding, makes a small cave on the north side of the cove. Comparison of the pattern of sedimentation on both sides of the cove shows that the throw of the fault is about 5 m.

The Aberystwyth District

On rounding the headland a large strike-slip fault, trending 095°, is seen in the beach platform (**Loc. 5**). Bending of the beds indicates seaward movement of the northern side and the lowest thick grit on the northern side can be identified nearly halfway up the cliff on the south. The horizontal separation is 80 m.

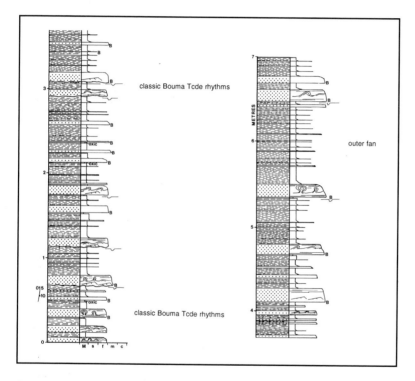

Figure 17: Log of the classic Aberystwyth Grits Formation taken at locality 4, Itinerary 5.

The beds can be traced along the bay northwards, with good examples of *Palaeodictyon* (a net-like trace fossil) and sedimentary structures visible at the base of the cliffs (Please do not remove these). Beyond the next headland the faulted syncline seen from the breakwater is well exposed. The fault is nearly vertical, and remarkable, steeply plunging folds and well developed small wavelength folds are seen at the base of the cliff immediately opposite the large stack. A double movement of the fault can be deduced.

The Aberystwyth District

Figure 18: Photograph of Constitution Hill showing the iron ladder and the position of the log site.

Beyond this, to the north, a large bedding plane surface dips seaward whilst just below this the three key beds are seen again.. Walk a short distance to the north, then turn to look at the form of the fold. It is, in general, periclinal with a central faulted zone, but is more complex that this statement implies. The change in degree of plunge is clear. The three key beds can easily be traced on the beach platform to the north, running obliquely towards the sea. However,

The Aberystwyth District

they can be found again, near the foot of the cliff in the second cove to the north of the large bedding plane, between the sea stack Cormorant Rock (**Loc. 6**) on the north side and the cliff, with the same dip as in the beach platform. This repetition is due to faulting parallel to the bedding, but it is difficult to find the fault plane, despite perfect exposure. In any inland exposure the fault would be impossible to trace.

Look now at Cormorant Rock itself. This landward-dipping sequence displays a transition from turbidites deposited under oxic conditions (with trace fossils) to anoxic conditions (smooth, flat bedding planes with rare graptolites). In the transitional zone pyritised burrows may be observed. 20 m to the N of Cormorant Rock rare brachiopods occur in the fallen blocks at the base of the cliff. It appears that the brachiopods may be confined to one bedding plane.

Up to about the Cormorant Rock the effect of the folding and faulting on the horizon of the beds has been practically nil, the three key beds being at the beach level as they are at Aberystwyth, though they are dipping the other way. It is, therefore, possible to identify any desired bed and observe the amount of lithological change with increasing distance from the promenade. Beyond this point, continuing towards Clarach, a steadily descending succession, about 140 m thick, is seen in the cliffs, below the three key beds. The turbidite sequence is dominated by Tde intervals with associated packets of Tcde. There is a marked disparity in the directions of palaeocurrents indicated by flute and cross-bedding respectively; indeed, directions indicated by the latter vary widely from bed to bed. These beds are indicative of an outer fan or basin-plain environment. Ripple drift bedding occurs, and many sole structures are well seen in fallen blocks. Neither amalgamated beds nor slumped beds occur, in strong contrast with the next section. A light coloured ash band, about 2 cm thick, runs up the cliff above a prominent cave as one enters Clarach Bay (**Loc. 7**), and is considered to be the northern exposure of the band recognised at Gilfach (Itinerary 2).

At the end of the section between 2 and 4 m of brown Head rests on solid rock. Clarach valley beyond shows a clearly parabolic profile; it is an alluvially-filled glaciated valley, cut well below present sea-level and subsequently filled. Its width and straightness testify to its importance in the glacial drainage pattern. The glacial sequence is better developed on the north side of the valley (see Itinerary 6).

Return to Aberystwyth by the path at the top of the cliff. Note the bevel along the edge of the cliff and the way in which its prolongation meets the outer edge of the beach platform below. Many of the faults and associated structures on the beach platform can be appreciated best from this height.

From the top of Constitution Hill overlooking Aberystwyth, the small patch of raised beach on which the castle stands, and that lying at the foot of Pen

The Aberystwyth District

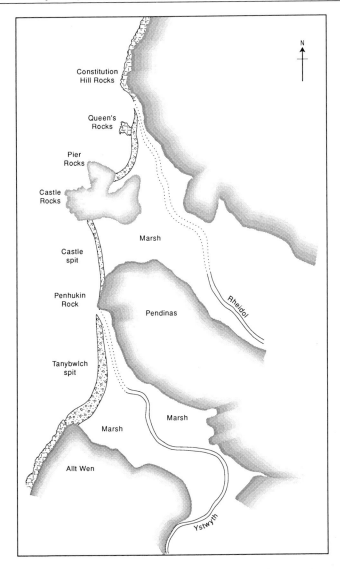

Figure 19: Principal geomorphic features in the Aberystwyth area prior to the building of the first castle in 1277 and extensive permanent human settlement. An earlier motte and bailey fort had been constructed close to the Ystwyth, whilst Pendinas was the site of an Iron Age fort. Shaded areas are land above 10 m.

The Aberystwyth District

Dinas, just beyond the town, can be observed. Before the development of permanent settlements and the building of the harbour, the Rheidol river drained through a sandy gravel spit that connected Constitution Hill to Castle Rocks (Figure 19). Likewise, the Ystwyth river drained through a similar sandy gravel spit that connected Castle Rocks to Allt Wen. The relative narrowness of the two river exits and the development of barrier spits, as a result of longshore drift, reduced the opportunity for the formation of true estuaries that are such a feature of the Cardigan Bay coastline.

6. CLARACH TO WALLOG, SN 586841 to 590857. Slumped beds, ripple drift bedding, correlation across folds and faults using 'patterns' of beds, relationships between folding and cleavage, and graptolites. Figures 20, 21 and 22. (M.R.D., D.K.L., W.R.F. & A.C.).

Drive to the beach along the road that branches left and westwards off the B4572 on the northern side of the Clarach stream. Note the shingle spit that extends across the valley entrance and diverts the stream discharge site to the north. Walk northwards, observing the Quaternary succession in the low cliffs close to Glan-y-Mor at **Loc. 1** (SN 58658427); it consists of 6 m of resedimented Welsh Blue Till, and 3 m of brown Head that contains about 8 sand and gravel beds in the sector close to Clarach valley. The weathered upper surface of the Aberystwyth Grits Formation dips steeply south, defining the north flank of the glacially overdeepened Clarach valley. Wave-cut rock platforms are present both to the north and south of the valley, but are absent across the entrance.

Examine the Silurian in a small tooth-like stack (**Loc. 1**), two metres high, lying between the beach platform and the first small headland. Here, a mudstone 60 cm thick is overlain by a slumped bed, to the top of which is welded a thin greywacke of variable thickness. In the mudstone there are eleven coarser grained partings, the 3rd and 9th being thicker than the others. This set of beds is easily recognisable and enables correlation to be made across folds and faults, both here and for a considerable distance to the north. A sharp plunging anticline and complementary syncline lie just to the east of the stack. Near the cliff in the centre of the bay the key mudstone and associated beds are seen again, and are obviously thicker. Here, graptolites may be found in many of the dark mudstone bands confirming that the sequence is part of Subzone 4a. In the headland to the north note how the uppermost beds have been shattered by deep frost action below the glacial head. Generally, the turbidite units, which are the same age as those observed at Aberystwyth , consist of Tde Bouma divisions, whilst at irregular intervals coarser sequences with fine sandstone beds (Tcde) and ripple cross-lamination occur. Ripple lee-slope orientation is variable from north through east. Thick beds containing mud flakes are prominent markers.

The Aberystwyth District

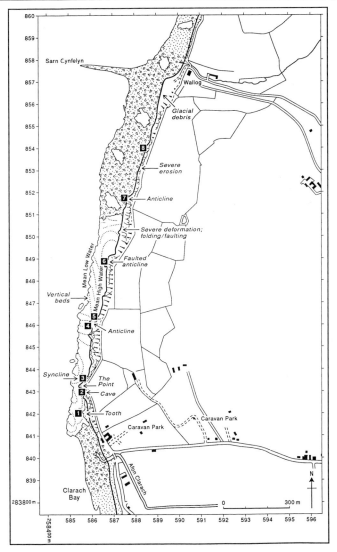

Figure 20: Location map for Itinerary 6, Clarach to Wallog. The rock platform close to locality 1 reveals the complexity of the small scale tectonics. Exposures such as these, with clearly defined small scale tectonic features, have been used to understand better the transpressional (oblique slip) phases of the Caledonian orogeny. The dotted lines on the foreshore indicate the general strike of the beds.

Pass round this headland into a small bay that contain a cave (**Loc. 2**). Three thick slumped beds can be seen on the right, almost equidistant from each other, with a fourth a greater distance above (Figure 21). Closely-spaced small flute casts occur on their bases, well seen in the roof of the cave, showing that the currents still had power to erode. The detailed lithology, both of the individual slumped beds and of associated strata, varies such that each can easily be identified in other exposures. The lower 7 or 10 cm of each bed is a typical graded greywacke; but the main part of the bed consists of a once slurried matrix with angular fragments of mudstone, and intraformational conglomerate, together with rounded patchy remnants of 'grit' layers. At the top there is evidence of current lamination and the top , like the base, is planar. These observations suggest that either each of these complex beds reflects repeated slope failure in the area to the south of Clarach with down-slope slumping, or *in situ* rapid dewatering followed an increase in contained water pressure as a result of high rates of sedimentation. Beds below the slumped beds can be successively studied at beach level in well polished surfaces. They include a thick, almost uniform greywacke with a laminated top, a thick bipartite bed with rippling between the two parts and subangular shale fragments in the lower half only, and two greywackes close together with an almost continuous layer of cone-in-cone nodules between. Less than 2 metres below the nodule layer well-formed load casts can be seen in the top of a thick grit. All these beds can be identified again to the north, by their relationship with the slumped beds, and variations in sedimentation observed. Examine the cliff face on the north side of the cove and compare it with the log (Figures 21 and 22).

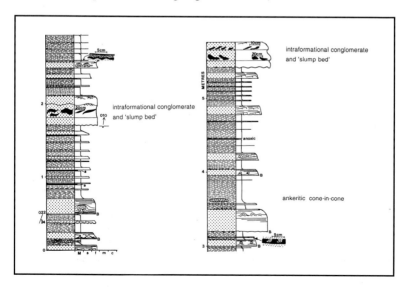

Figure 21: Log of the rocks seen at location 2, Itinerary 6.

The Aberystwyth District

Figure 22: Photograph of the log site. The height of the cliff face shown is about 15 m; here the thicker 'slumped beds' are readily identified. Use the log to judge the thickness of individual slumped beds.

Tectonically, this section displays examples of repeated or progressive folding and associated cleavage. Cleavage transects some folds, is axial-planar in others and in places is itself folded. An example of an anticline transected by cleavage occurs on the wave-cut platform at SN 58528432 close to **Loc. 2**. Many of the folds have metre-scale wavelengths and are tight structures with generally N-S upright axial planes. Two phases of folding are often recognisable; one with a N-S trend and a later one with a NNW - SSE trend. Two interpretations of the complex relationships between folds and cleavage are: 1) accommodation in the core of a major anticline, 2) progressive deformation during regional transpression.

Walk around 'The Point' to the north (SN 58548433), only possible at low spring tides, and into a small embayment, where ripple drift bedding (climbing ripples) occurs at beach level, Continue on to a fault cleft in the cliffs, observing various sedimentary structures and folding. Looking back, a syncline **(Loc. 3)** can be seen in the lower part of the cliff, overlain by almost undisturbed beds. This structure is clearly of tectonic origin, movement having been taken up by a bedding plane slip at the base of the undisturbed beds.

Walk towards the next headland (SN 58598460), passing through a narrow gap in southward dipping beds. An elongate syncline orientated NNW - SSE

The Aberystwyth District

occurs on the platform between the two headlands and may be viewed from the cliff-top path. In the embayment the key beds reappear; significantly the key mudstone now measures 90 cm in thickness. Note that the greywacke above the slumped bed is now partly separated from it by mudstone. This is considered to be evidence of lessened erosive power of the current as the distance from the source increased and the palaeoslope was replaced by a flat sea floor. In the headland (**Loc. 4**), which contains a blow-hole, the slumped beds are present, whilst the previously mentioned beds can all be identified down to the two grits with cone-in-cone nodules between them. Remarkable cone-in-cone nodules elongated in the direction of cleavage are visible at beach level about 8 metres north of the headland. In the northward facing cliff strong folds and faulting are seen, and on the beach platform a small perfect periclinal fold with one vertical limb illustrates the form of the folds.

Immediately to the north of the headland (**Loc. 5**) there occurs a major shear zone thought to be caused by dextral wrench faulting. Beyond, the beds strike nearly parallel to the cliffs and dip steeply (between 60 and 75 degrees) inland. Near a tiny cove the four slumped beds, here much thinner, can be identified again, with a raft of mudstone, 3 metres long and upside down, in the fourth slumped bed. In the small embayment the key beds can be traced, and on the north side note the variation in type of mudstone, with very thin deep black layers separating broader bands of differing grey colours. The beds can be followed to the next headland (SN 58668486, **Loc. 6**), where reversed or high angle thrust faulting and an anticline are seen. Beyond this is a zone of tectonic complexity involving both faulting and folding in which first one, and then another of the slumped beds can be identified in the beach exposures. The key beds can be picked up for the last time in the larger of the last two sea stacks. Here, the beds dip seawards and the greywacke above the slumped bed has a plane base and has not succeeded in cutting through the mudstone below. If one follows these beds they are seen to turn round the nose of a steeply plunging anticline on the beach platform. On the other limb of the fold both greywackes and mudstones are much thinner. The mudstone is reduced to 45 cm and the basal grit band is markedly thinned. On the headland note the small scale folds that can be closely examined.

North of SN 85105870, the rock platform is largely covered by shingle, which persists as far as Wallog. At SN 5878 8519 (**Loc. 7**) a NNW orientated anticline may be seen in the cliff. For 300 m northwards the modern cliff is nearly on the line of a pre-till cliff, cut during a period of climatic amelioration. The beach platform, in consequence, is cut across till and rock outcrops are rare. The upper surface of the rock exposure in the cliff can be seen to slope towards the narrow Wallog valley (**Loc. 8**). A series of gravel beds, collectively 8 m thick, are overlain by 7 to 10 metres of Head, ending with a loess-like layer just below the soil. Wallog lies on a soliflucted smoothed platform of glacial deposits. Here too is the famous Sarn Cynfelyn (Welsh—sarnau, singular sarn, meaning causeway) extending as an exposed cobble ridge 400 metres from the beach at low tide. The ridge is one of several extending into Cardigan Bay and inferred to be glacial medial moraines of piedmont glaciers moving down the Welsh valleys. This particular Sarn continues underwater for 11 km. It can be assumed that prior to the post-glacial rise in sea-level and attendant marine erosion the overall height of the Sarn approached that of the adjacent cliffs (see Appendix 2 and Figures 45 and 46). The cobbles and pebbles of the sarn are dominantly of local derivation although there also several cobbles derived from the the Ordovician Aran Volcanics exposed in southern Snowdonia and also smaller pebbles from Irish Sea Till, presumably transported northwards by longshore and beach drift.

Return to Clarach by way of the cliff-top path although care is necessary as erosion frequently makes the path unsafe. From the cliff-top folding and faulting displayed in the wave-cut platform may be readily observed.

7. WALLOG TO HARP ROCK, SN 590857. Distal facies, sole markings, regular banding, amalgamated beds, internal rippling of beds, graptolites. Figures 23, 24 and 25. (M.R.D., D.K.L. & A.C.).

Take the coast road from Aberystwyth to Borth (B4572). Two kilometres north of Llangorwen take the lane to the beach, at an inconspicuous cross-roads just before a steep hill. Park after turning; it is not possible to take a car to the beach. Walk down the lane to the beach, cross the stream by a small bridge and descend on the north side of a waterfall to the beach. Here (**Loc. 1**) Pleistocene conglomerate beds 5 m thick rest directly on the Silurian strata. They in turn are overlain by up to 5 m of Head.

In the low cliffs on each side of the stream there is a prominent three layered bed, about 40 cm thick consisting of a greywacke base, slurried middle and a very fine grained upper layer. This is a key bed and will be seen for some considerable distance northward, across a number of folds and thrusts. Indeed, much of this part of the first section is aligned parallel to the strike with the beds dipping to the east at about 20 degrees. The key bed is unusually thick for this distal site which, unlike Aberystwyth and Clarach, is of Subzone 3 age (Figure 1). 50 m to the N a high-angle 1 m wide shear zone (**Loc. 2**) may be the site of a thrust.

Walk to the sea's edge and view the solifluction plateau as a whole. On the left the coastal bevel lies above a considerable cliff and can be seen to run round behind the cultivated fields. The glacial deposits are mantling a

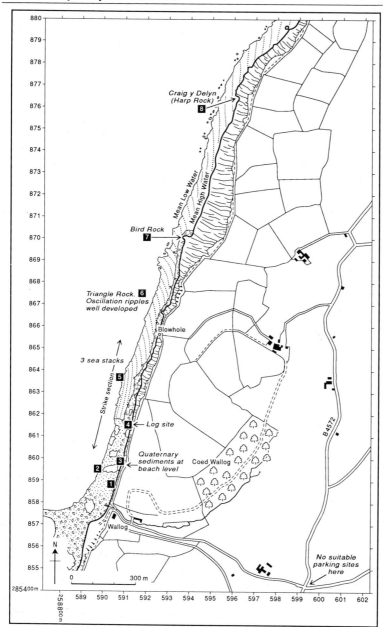

Figure 23: Location map for Itinerary 7, Wallog to Harp Rock.

The Aberystwyth District

raised platform, later deeply dissected, and glacial beds descend to below high tide mark along an old valley (**Loc. 3**). Two sequences of channel gravels can be observed (Figure 47).

Proceed northwards along the beach, noting the amalgamated beds with coarser base and finer top portion. Also along this section the soles of the beds are well displayed. It is at **Loc. 4** that the graphic log (Figure 24) was made. Note the uniformity of thickness of even the thinnest light coloured layers, and their lateral persistence, also the regular nature of the fine banding, seen even more strikingly some distance to the north. These features are all exceptionally well displayed near the headland behind the three sea stacks. One bed with prominent trace fossils on the base can be traced for several hundred metres. The triple bed is visible in the middle of the sea stack nearest the cliff.

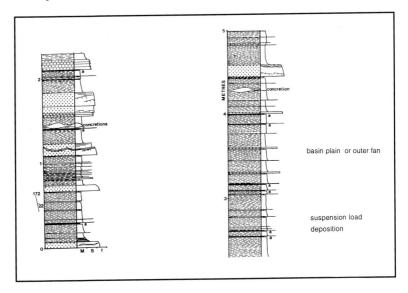

Figure 24: Log of the rocks seen at locality 4, Itinerary 7, immediately N of Wallog.

Behind the headland by the three stacks (**Loc. 5**) a high angle fault is seen, which runs obliquely across the beach platform, and seems to throw the beds seawards, though the dip remains to the east. The character of sedimentation changes subtly, the proportion of mudstone is greater, good grading is seen, and some of the amalgamated beds show internal rippling between two portions. The mudstones, well seen at beach level immediately round the next headland, show evidence of turbidity current transport and very thin black bands occur,

The Aberystwyth District

deposited as true pelagic mud. These contain graptolites. It is easier, however, to see these further N, to the S of Harp Rock.

Continue towards the triangular sea stack (**Loc. 6**) in the distance, noting the strikingly regular spacing of the thin greywacke bands. About two thirds of the distance from the last headland to the sea stack the upper surfaces of the beds in the beach platform, close to the cliff, are ripple marked with the ripple crests striking eastwards towards the sea. They are transverse to the current direction as deduced from sole markings. Close inspection will show that the topmost layer of each bed has been eroded off, to display the ripples. The wavelength is consistently 42 cm whilst the symmetry of form suggests they are oscillation ripples. As the depositional site is well below wave and storm base, oscillation ripples of this type may be associated with instabilities along the upper flow boundary of the turbidity current and seen as internal waves.

About 60 metres north of the triangular stack incomplete specimens of *Palaeodictyon*, ridges bifurcating at regular angles, but not joining up to make a regular meshwork, occur on the base of a bed in the cliff. At the stack itself, good transverse ripples can be seen on the upper surfaces of beds in the beach platform.

Just behind the stack and slightly to the northward, is a faulted syncline. The beds gradually flatten out, and north of a small waterfall the triple bed first noticed on reaching the beach at Wallog is seen again. Details of sedimentation in this and associated beds are clearly visible. The thickness of mudstone between the light coloured bands is greater than at Wallog. Good rippling between the two parts of an amalgamated bed is seen in the first 15 cm graywacke above the triple bed.

These beds can be studied in any desired detail as far as the next low headland. Here in the cliff above, beds dip steeply seaward, and the axis of this overthrust syncline (**Loc. 7**) is visible on the north side of the headland. If the syncline is traced along the beach to the north it is found to diminish in amplitude. The complementary anticline to the east is unfaulted, though on looking back a fault can be seen along its crests to the south. The fold is periclinal, dying out in both directions, and arranged *en echelon* with the well defined syncline at the foot of Harp Rock in the distance. This spectacular fold likewise can be seen to run up the cliff and die out southwards. The triple bed is seen for the last time dipping seaward, on the east side of the syncline, about 200 metres north of the low headland. Here the central portion contains many angular chips of mudstone. This and all the associated beds are noticeably thicker. Harp Rock (**Loc. 8**) marks the northern limit of exposure of the Aberystwyth Grits Formation; beyond lies the Borth Mudstones Formation (see Itinerary 8). To the S of Harp Rock it is possible to observe, and collect if desired, graptolites from fallen blocks of Aberystwyth Grits Formation. Preservation is as low relief pyrite internal moulds. Several different species

The Aberystwyth District

Figure 25: Photograph of Harp Rock (about 22 m high) looking N; to the right on the landward side is the Borth Mudstones Formation; to the left on the seaward side is the Aberystwyth Grits Formation.

are present, some of the monograptaceous (particularly the subzonal index species, *Pristiograptus renaudi,*) attaining considerable length.

Return to Wallog along the beach or, if desired, continue past Harp Rock to Aberwennal Bay, past a confused and difficult section, where the presence of periclinal folds can again be demonstrated. It is then possible to return to Wallog along the top of the cliffs whence fine views of the steeply dipping beds of Harp Rock can be obtained.

8. BORTH TO HARP ROCK, SN 60738887. Very distal basin plain mudstones, trace fossils and quartz veining. Figure 26. (M.R.D. & D.K.L.)

Travel north from Aberystwyth on the A487 and turn left at Rhyd-y-pennau on to the B4343 to Borth. The Borth Mudstones Formation is exposed in the cliffs and shore platform just south of the road junction in Upper Borth. Cars can be parked adjacent to the beach both south and north of the road junction. Walk southwest along the base of the cliffs towards Harp Rock (Craig y Delyn).

The rocks exposed from Borth to Harp Rock are predominantly mudstones and considered in the past to be both lithologically distinct from the

The Aberystwyth District

Aberystwyth Grits Formation and older. Modern studies using graptolites have demonstrated that, in fact, they are the same age (subzones 2 and 3) as the AGF sediments exposed at New Quay and Cei Bach and consist simply of the distal portion of the same turbidite fan. Therefore, when examining this section it is important that these mudstones are seen as part of a single depositional environment extending from at least New Quay in the south to the Dovey estuary in the north (Figure 2).

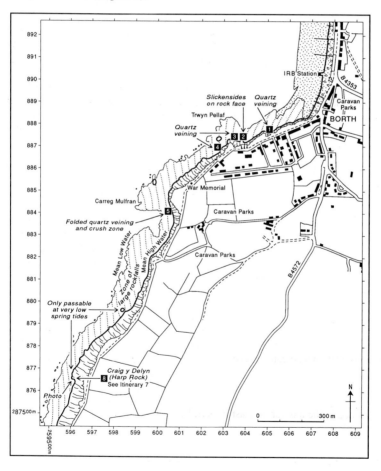

Figure 26: Location map for Itinerary 8, Borth to Harp Rock . The dotted lines on the foreshore indicate the general strike of the beds. Details of the relationships between folding, faulting and quartz veining may be studied along this part of the coast.

The Aberystwyth District

The cliffs from Borth to Harp Rock consist of Tde turbidite units, of which the Td portion is between 2 and 4 cm thick whilst the Te portion varies from 15 to 30 cm in thickness. Te beds when present are usually only a few centimetres thick, and occur more frequently in the higher parts of the Borth Mudstones further south. Sole structures, in the form of flutes, are sparse whilst *Palaeodictyon* is common.

For the first 300 m at least four anticlines and intervening synclines are crossed. Dips on the limbs are uniform; beds either strike towards 010 degrees and are vertical, younging to the west, or strike towards 030 degrees and dip at moderate angles to the southeast. Cleavage is strongly developed in the vertical limbs, but is not seen in the other limbs since it is parallel to the bedding. Several gullies are marked by transverse faults and prominent quartz veining (**Loc. 1, 3, 4, & 5**). A large southwest orientated face displays (**Loc. 2**) well developed slickensides. Of note is the width of the rock platform from the promenade south to beyond Harp Rock. On average the platform exceeds 150 m, which is twice the width seen at Aberarth, a fact that may reflect the vulnerability of the Borth Mudstones Formation to marine erosion.

The mudstone dominated sequence is considered to have been deposited in a outer fan-fringe to basin-plain environment. Low density, low energy and unconfined turbidity flows, transporting silt and clay, deposited sediment very slowly. A significant proportion of Te was hemipelagic sediment, and, where conditions on the sea floor were oxic, a rich benthic fauna developed. Thicker graptolite hemipelagites than have been encountered within the Aberystwyth Grits Formation to the S testify to prolonged periods of anoxicity and suggest that turbidity current incursions into the area at this time were less frequent than during deposition of the younger subzones of the Aberystwyth Grits Formation.

The boundary between the Aberystwyth Grits Formation and the Borth Mudstones Formation has been placed at the base of the oldest massive bed displayed in Harp Rock (**Loc. 8** of Itinerary 7 and Figure 25), where a distinct lithological change can be recognised. This lithological boundary does not coincide with the Subzone 3 and 4a biostratigraphical boundary which lies stratigraphically a short distance above. The real question is why there should be such a pronounced lithological change in an otherwise conformable sequence? The answer, at least in part, lies in the evidence available for the whole fan given below.

The Aberystwyth Turbidite Fan Reviewed. (M.R.D.). Figure 43.

Refinement of the graptolite biostratigraphy for the early Silurian (upper Llandovery, Telychian Stage, see Appendix 1), with the establishment of graptolite subzones, has allowed the patterns of sedimentation of the

The Aberystwyth District

Aberystwyth Grits and Borth Mudstones Formations to be re-examined for the first time since the classic paper by Wood and Smith in 1959. This high resolution biostratigraphy provides the framework for the application of detailed facies analysis techniques and an assessment of the probable impact on the development of the whole fan of variables such as sediment supply, eustatic sea-level changes and tectonic activity.

There are limitations, however. The biostratigraphical boundaries are not precise, because of the incompleteness of the graptolite record due to oxic conditions at the sea floor at various times during deposition which inhibited the preservation of organic matter. Despite these limitations the fan sediments can be broadly sub-divided and the proximal to distal sediments correlated. Further correlation support is provided by an ash band. A 4 cm thick band is recognised at Gilfach in subzone 4a and a 2 cm band at Clarach, again in subzone 4a.

Fan development, as seen at New Quay in west Wales, commenced with rapid, localised, coarse grained lobe progradation that was succeeded by abandonment reflecting a decline in sediment supply (Subzone 2 and most of 3). Subsequent resumption of sediment supply, that was gradual at first then pronounced, promoted further lobe progradation which, in turn, was succeeded by gradual retrogression (Subzone 4a and b). Apart from the initial phase of progradation, attributed to tectonic uplift in the supply area (what is now Pembrokeshire), the early development of the submarine fan system is consistent with what is now known about eustatic sea-level changes during the early Silurian and determined from sites elsewhere in Europe and Asia. In addition, local basin tectonics, which affected the patterns of sedimentation and initiated syn-sedimentary deformation, are now seen to have played a major role in the overall form of the submarine fan system.

Using the biostratigraphical framework as the control, fan-wide facies boundaries can be sought for. The most important boundaries are those recognised as unconformities, which are most clearly identified in upper fan sequences. Upper fan unconformities record the important sea-level lowstands or episodes of regression. Unfortunately, the upper fan sequence in west Wales has been lost through erosion. Apart from the existence of erosive bases associated with turbidity current activity, most notable at the base of the thick sandstone sequence at Aberarth, no unconformities are recognised along the entire section from New Quay to Borth.

In the absence of unconformities, sharp facies changes within the lower fan, that mark major shifts or changes in sedimentation (equivalent to upper fan unconformities) which are not simply progradations, but may reflect tectonic, and/or sea-level influences, need to be assessed. The most important facies shift along the whole outcrop occurs at the Aberystwyth Grits Formation-Borth Mudstones Formation lithological boundary located towards the top of subzone

The Aberystwyth District

3 at Harp Rock (Itinerary 8). Here, a sequence characterised by the presence of greywacke intervals conformably overlies predominantly mudstones facies. This lithological boundary lies stratigraphically below the ash band marker. A similar although less well marked facies change occurs along the Cei Bach to Gilfach section, again below the prominent ash band. This down-fan lithological shift reflects a sudden increase in sediment supply and whilst uplift of the provenance area might be an explanation, as in Subzone 2, a more likely cause is a eustatic fall in sea-level. If the patterns of sedimentation observed for the fan as a whole can be related to a fall in sea-level then patterns should be present that might indicate a transgressional phase. Transgression phases cause restrictions in sediment supply and the formation of condensed sequences followed by shale-prone deposits. Interestingly, condensed sequences occur in Subzone 5, whilst Subzone 6 above, is markedly shale-prone. But, if the fan does indeed record a regression-transgression cycle, what is the time scale involved?

In terms of duration the Telychian Stage lasted about 2.2 million years, equivalent to 8 graptolite biozones. That part ascribed to the AGF-BMF is about 2 graptolite biozones or between 500,000 and 1.5 million years, but note that graptolite biozones are not of equal duration. This length of time might usefully be considered to equate to a 4th order eustatic transgression-regression cycle. Sea-level cycles are classified according to duration such that 3rd order cycles are between 1 and 5 million years and 4th order cycles have durations of hundreds of thousands of years. Thus, in brief, the stratal patterns recognised for the fan as a whole include:-

1. Facies boundary located towards the top of Subzone 3 and seen as due to a regressive phase.
2. Slope and basin fan build-out equivalent to Subzone 4a and 4b when the shelf was exposed.
3. Condensed sequence interpreted as due to a transgressive phase seen as Subzone 5.
4. Deep water conditions (maximum transgression) seen as shale prone and locally anoxic, seen as Subzones 6, 7 and c (*crispus*, see Appendix 1).

But what about the coarse grained sequences at New Quay of Subzone 2 age? Note that the lateral equivalents are the Borth Mudstones Formation. Firstly, there must have been a period of rapid sedimentation dominated by amalgamated beds. Hence, sediment supply was high and might be the result of uplift in the source area. Secondly, the rapid deposition may reflect sudden loss of slope momentum with the finer suspension load carried 45 km across the basin floor. Abrupt changes in slope suggest that the southern margin of the Welsh basin was fault controlled. Thirdly, following the effect of tectonics on sediment supply, subsequent events were under the influence of sea-level changes, seen as lobe progradation after the relatively quiet period of Subzone 3 and possibly lobe switching as recognised in Subzone 6 at Monk's Cave.

The Aberystwyth District

Thus, whilst it is not possible to establish a full sequence equivalent to a regressive-transgressive cycle most of the components are present. As more supporting biostratigraphic data becomes available it might be possible to refine this essentially simple model.

Modern Sedimentary Environments

Geologists study modern environments of deposition to understand sedimentary rocks better . The maxim that the present is the key to the past holds especially well for sediment studies as does the rule which states that subenvironments occurring side by side will be preserved in a vertical sequence in the rock record as a result of subsidence and sea-level changes. This concept is termed Walther's Law. Understanding depositional processes and the role of flora and fauna allows the environment as a whole to be better appreciated and modelled. The following itineraries are concerned with two marginal marine environments.

9. THE DOVEY ESTUARY. Tidal flats, including fauna and flora and sedimentation processes, fossil forest. Figures 27 and 28. (M.R.D. & J.R.H.).

This itinerary can only be undertaken at low spring tides with appropriate equipment including wellington boots and ideally a small spade. Take the A487 to Tre'r-ddol and turn left on to the B4353. Drive as far as the first bend and park near a ford (SN 654929) about 500 m down a lane that branches off the B4353. Walk to the railway using the track that runs along the side of the canalised Clettwr river. With care cross the railway east of the bridge over the Clettwr. From the railway line walk northwards across the high marsh.

The high marsh is covered by water only during spring tides and the highest parts only by exceptionally high tides. It is separated from the low marsh by a small cliff which approximates to the mean level of spring tides. This part of the marsh is characterised by dense vegetation. Salt pans occur only occasionally in the upper high marsh, but where they do they are large, long lived (more than 30 years), up to 6 m in diameter and about 45 cm deep. During the last 60 years the low marsh has been extensively colonised by *Spartina townsendii*. This vigorous hybrid has penetrated into the sward along the connecting channels and is now well established in many of the pans, especially around the margins. The deposits of the high marsh are clayey silts with about 15% fine sand. In profile, brown iron hydroxide, grey monosulphide and black bisulphide zones can be seen. Well digested *Phragmites* peat occurs as 10 cm layers locally. The fauna of the high marsh is extremely limited, molluscs are absent, whilst foraminifera are restricted to arenaceous forms which construct a protective shell-like structure from sand grains. This general absence of fauna is attributed to the long periods of exposure and drying between high spring tides. The pans of the sward show a

The Aberystwyth District

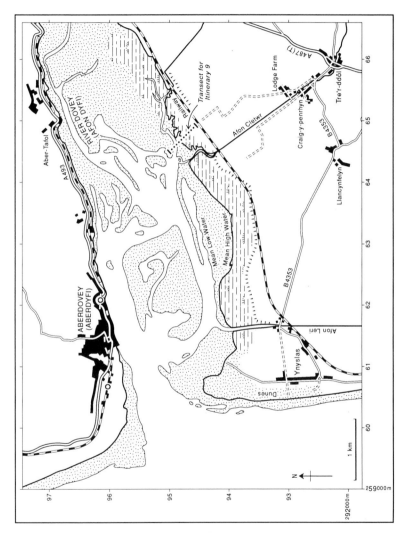

Figure 27: Location map for the Dovey (Dyfi) Estuary transect for Itinerary 9. Note the site of Ynyslas which is part of Itinerary 10. Lined areas above mean high water represent the high marsh or tidal flats only covered by spring tides; stippled areas enclose the low marsh or low tidal flats including the sand flats. The area immediately south of the railway line is mainly freshwater fen, and reclaimed pasture.

The Aberystwyth District

much more varied living fauna because of the channel connections with the low marsh. Hence they exhibit an extension of the low marsh fauna including shrimps and fish. The green alga *Enteromorpha* is widely developed in the summer.

The low marsh is completely covered by all high tides except the smallest neaps. The original flora described in 1916 by Yapp and Jones has been largely replaced by *Spartina* which has also actively invaded the edges of the open flats. In the summer this plant reaches 1 m in height. Moreover, it has promoted silting and the general buildup of the lower marsh. The deposits of the low marsh display a considerable range of composition from clayey silts to sediments largely composed of fine sand. In profile the sediments are finely laminated reflecting seasonal variations (during the summer *Enteromorpha* effectively traps fine-grained sediment, forming organic-rich laminae). The laminae are commonly spaced as widely as 20 cm. At depth the laminations are replaced by structureless sands with shell fragments. Bands of iron deposits, that are probably the result of bacterial activity. occur within the lower marsh.

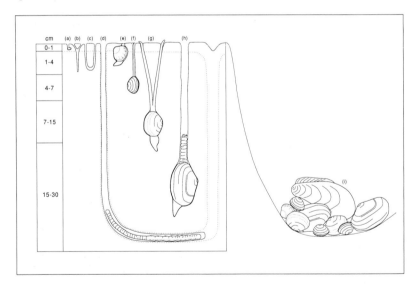

Figure 28: Infauna of the Dovey Estuary; (a) Hydrobia, (b) Polychaete, (c) Corophium burrow, (d) Arenicola, (e) Cardium, (f) Macoma, (g) Scrobiculavia, (h) Mya, (i) Mytilus. With permission redrawn and modified from Open University publication S334 Unit 10. Note the collection of shells on the right represents disarticulated and lagged shell material on the floor of a tidal creek and utilised as a hard substrate by the edible mussel Mytilus.

The Aberystwyth District

As the low marsh tends to be waterlogged at low tide it has the richest fauna in the estuary. Use the diagram provided (Figure 28), and with careful observation and a small spade try to identify the variety of types present. The infauna, that is all those animals that burrow into or are buried within the sediment, includes *Mya*, also known as 'Gapers' because the siphons are almost permanently extended. Two main species are found in the Dovey: *Mya arenaria*, the sand gaper, and *Mya truncata*, the blunt gaper. They live at about 30 cm depth, are inactive and have long siphons in a protective sheath; they are suspension feeders. The common *Scrobicularia piperita* is a deposit feeder and lives at a depth of about 12 cm. Again it uses siphons, two in this case, an exhalent siphon and an inhalent siphon that makes radial trace patterns on the sediment surface. *Macoma balthica* has a similar habit, but prefers slightly higher salinities. Its shell is pink to crimson. *Cerastoderma (Cardium,)* the common edible cockle, lives just below the sediment-water interface and is a suspension or filter feeder. All these are lamellibranch or bivalve molluscs, and can be observed in life position if a shallow pit is dug at a site where syphon holes occur at the surface. *Hydrobia*, however, is a tiny gastropod which burrows into the muddy surface, whilst another gastropod *Littorina* travels over the mud, and also climbs the *Spartina*. Worms are common and amphipods occur widely with the burrows of *Corophium* existing at densities of up to 1 per square cm. Foraminifera and ostracods are also very common. (Note that ducks eat mainly epifauna, shelducks mainly *Hydrobia*, waders with short bills eat shallow burrowers, long-billed oyster catchers search for the deep burrowers).

The low marsh is dissected by a network of creeks or narrow channels. Many of the channels show active headwater erosion and can be up to 2 m deep. Where the channels pass through the low marsh they are often choked with banks of disarticulated shells including *Scrobicularia* and *Mya*. These genera may be seen in positions of growth in the exposed silts in the channel walls. Some of the shell banks are colonised by the edible mussel *Mytilus edulis*. Lateral channel migration results in the formation of point bars, whilst scouring the muds has also resulted in the building of prominent levees on either bank. Sediments near the channels tend to retain air as a result of the disparity in the ratio of the rise of the water table to the rise of the tidal water; this results in cavities forming within the sediment. The resemblance of the marsh channels and gullies to the Main Channel only holds for the lower part of their courses where they cross the sand flats.

Beyond the marsh lies the open sand flats, the most extensive physiographical unit; it is too unstable to support vegetation. Although the open sand flats are covered by all high tides, drainage is rapid and on occasion the dried surface is reworked by the wind. Only a few macroscopic life forms are adapted to this hostile environment, chiefly worms, especially *Arenicola* and the active filter feeding mollusc *Cerastoderma (Cardium) edule*. The

The Aberystwyth District

sediments of this environment are medium to fine-grained sands containing abundant shell fragments. Where the Main Channel has eroded into the sand flats depositional structures are exposed, usually in the form of crude laminations. Mixed wave and current activity has produced a great complex of ripple forms that appear to cover the sand flats completely when viewed at low water springs. The most frequent form is the asymmetrical small scale ripple, which displays long straight crests, low amplitudes of 1 to 2 cm and wavelengths of 10 cm. As observation is restricted to low water most of the bed forms are ebb orientated. Current oscillations appear to be responsible for modifying the crest of asymmetrical ripples by creating troughs that can be traced along the original crest line of the ripples. Lingoid (tongue shaped) ripples appear infrequently on the sand flats and only near the Main Channel margin. The large scale ripples, here called mega-ripples, even though wave height rarely exceeds 1 m, are located along the margin of the Main Channel.

In the Main Channel environment water cover is continuous. The sediment is the same as that on the sand flats, and the structures are a continuation of those described earlier. Mega-ripples cover the entire length of the Main Channel. Vegetation is absent and micro- and macro-fauna consists of current swept dead forms derived both from the marshes and Cardigan Bay.

The fossil forest can be seen at low tide in the channel of the Clettwr where it has cut down through the latest marsh succession (since its course was altered in the 19th century).

Retrace your steps back to the railway and thence to the track.

10. YNYSLAS FORESHORE, fossil forest, sand and shingle spit and dune field and shell collecting. Figure 29. (M.R.D. & J.R.H.).

Drive along the B4353 north from Borth as far as the road junction known as Ynyslas Turn (SN 607925). Turn left along the gravel track and cross the golf course to the car park. Walk across to the shingle ridge which consists of cobbles and pebbles. Most of the clasts are tabulate in shape and of local Welsh derivation having been reworked from the Welsh Till. The ridge extends, from the low (20 m) cliffs at Borth in the south, northwards from a distance of about 5 km; it reaches a height of 5 m above O.D. and a width of 60 m. At the northern end of the ridge lies an extensive dune field. From the top of the shingle ridge it is possible to see part of the original course of the river (afon) Leri; it can be traced north, for a distance of 3 km, from Borth railway station across the golf course to Ynyslas Turn. A line of reed beds marks the line of the old course. According to early editions of the Ordnance Survey the site of the river mouth for the period 1824 to 1871 was close to Ynyslas Turn (SN 920605); subsequently the river was diverted and today flows in an artificial channel northwards to the Dovey (Dyfi) estuary. The old Leri river

The Aberystwyth District

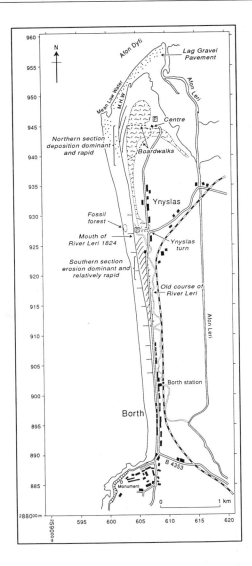

Figure 29: Location map for Itinerary 10, Borth to Ynyslas. Note the area with the curved symbol in the north, and crossed by the boardwalks, is the Ynyslas dune field. The short lines shown immediately south of the 1824 mouth of the river Leri represent the numerous recurved spit terminations. Afon is the Welsh word for river.

The Aberystwyth District

course can be seen to cross the B4353 between the fenced-in house to the south and the gravel track; it runs towards the car park and northwards parallel with the shingle ridge.

Close to the northern limit of the old river course (immediately southeast of the car park) about 10 recurved shingle spit ridges can be recognised. Indeed, much of the golf course, to the west of the road, is developed across recurved spit terminations that extend northwards from SN 608910. Note the present-day shingle ridge consists of a base of rounded cobbles, that may ultimately form a lag pavement, a lower berm of fine pebbles and a ridge top consisting of tabulate cobbles. These tabulate cobbles have an imbricate stacking pattern.

Following diversion of the river Leri the shingle ridge extended rapidly northwards (Figure 29) to within 400 m of the estuary. The curvilinear shape of the ridge is the result of erosion and eastward migration of the beach south of SN 605920 and active deposition to the north. Extensive lag gravel pavements on the lower foreshore and linked to the northern limit of the present shingle ridge (SN 60549442), persist as far as the estuary mouth.

The evidence available suggests that the whole spit evolved close to its present position rather then having migrated eastwards with rising sea-level. Thus, during the rapid sea-level rise between 4000 and 5000 years ago, a shingle ridge probably developed at the western end of the Sarn, as deduced from the offshore sample data, but did not subsequently migrate eastwards. Certainly the Sarn to the S could have acted as a barrier to northward movement of sediment under the influence of longshore drift. Thus, the spit at Borth may have evolved in historical times.

Cross the shingle ridge to the beach. When shifting beach sands allow, a small area of fossil forest can be examined (SN 60459285), although traces occur along a 4 km stretch of the foreshore as far as Borth. It consists of prostrate trunks and stumps up to 60 cm in diameter with roots in position of growth in peat and marsh clays (*Scrobicularia* Clays of the previous marsh cycle). The dominant species are pine and birch; in some cases the bark can be clearly seen; oak is found in the south. Radiocarbon dates of approximately 6100 years BP give an Atlantic age for the forest or towards the end of the climatic optimum, although trees continued to flourish from 5200 to 4800 BP, thereafter they rapidly declined to be replaced by fen. The average age of the largest trunks is between 150 and 200 years. Although the oldest preserved trees occur in the north they persisted longer in the south. On rare occasions, as in 1968, when the entire lower shore was washed clear of sand, the forest is exposed right up to the cliffs at Borth, allowing the recovery of well preserved bones of *Bos primigenius* (Aurock). On these occasions too, interesting slump and compaction structures can be observed in the underlying clays.

Shell enthusiasts can make a representative collection of bivalves and gastropods washed in from the floor of Cardigan Bay including *Arctica islandica*, *Buccinum undulatum*, and various species of *Venus* and *Donax*.

The Aberystwyth District

Beach infauna include razor shells like *Solen* and *Ensis* and the gastropod *Natica*. In addition, boring bivalves like *Pholas* inhabit the peat beds. Finally, far travelled shells from outer Cardigan Bay include *Pecten, Glycimeris* and *Chlamys,* the Queen's scallop.

The Ynyslas dune field is developed north of the car park, in part across the estuarine clays, and consists of pyramidal to northeasterly orientated sand dunes with intervening hollows or slacks. Towards the north the beach consists of a series of linear sand bars that at low tide are exposed to the onshore winds which readily deflate them. When a strong onshore wind is blowing note, in particular, the sand streamers that extend up the beach towards the dunes. Sand grains and small shell fragments are transported across the beach to nourish the Ynyslas dunes; very fine grains are carried up the estuary. As the region is one of high rainfall, vegetation, in the form of grass, quickly colonises the dunes loosely stabilising them and promoting their irregular pyramidal form. Where the internal structure of a dune is revealed, large scale trough cross-bedding may be observed. In addition, it is instructive to examine the grain texture of the dunes and compare it with that of the beach. On the beach a wide range of grain sizes occurs, whereas the dunes are composed of a narrow grain size range with a mean of 0.3 mm. Based on evidence for sediment movement in the vicinity of Harlech castle, to the north, the dunes at Ynyslas may, as with the spit, have a short history; perhaps less than 800 years!

Where the circular boardwalk extends to the beach (SN 60459371) three terminal shingle ridges may be observed. Walk up the boardwalk to the viewpoint (SN 60559375) where the pattern of dune development can be appreciated. Either return to the road by way of the National Nature Reserve Information Centre using the boardwalk or walk further north along the shingle spit to its termination (SN 60549442) and then take another boardwalk (SN 60509420) across the dune field to the Information Centre and return to the car park along the access road.

Quaternary and Solid Geology of Cardigan Bay

The maximum Late Devensian ice advance occured about 18,000 years ago and deglaciation was completed by 14,000 BP; by 12,000 BP the climate of Wales was similar to that of the present day. Land-based Welsh ice developed initially from cirque glaciers that coalesced to form valley glaciers; subsequently large ice caps evolved. An ice cap in Wales, the core of which lay E of the Rhinog mountains, was an ice dispersal centre, as was the Plynlimon Dome in mid-Wales. These ice caps depressed the crust, particularly during the glacial maximum which occurred between 18,000 and 20,000 years BP when sea-level was between 40 and 45 m below the present level. The subsequent eustatic sea-level rise was rapid compared with the isostatic rebound. As a consequence glaciomarine conditions obtained in

The Aberystwyth District

Cardigan Bay, followed by a marine regression caused by the later rise of the crust (see Appendix 2). Despite vigorous valley glacier flow W towards Cardigan Bay pathways beyond the coast were blocked by the advancing Irish Sea Ice (Figure 45).

Although the Dovey valley glacier transported turbiditic sandstones clasts into Cardigan Bay the most distinctive erratics are the acid tuffs of Ordovician age from the Aran mountains; these may be collected from the beaches S of the Dovey estuary. Exotic erratics may also be collected, but only from particular locations along the coast (Itinerary 12); these have come from the floor of Cardigan Bay (Figure 48) and from as far afield as Scotland largely as a result of the erosive and transporting power of the Irish Sea Ice.

Although the Holocene or postglacial period commenced only 10,000 years ago reworking and erosion of the glacial deposits in the Welsh valleys was initiated by melt water streams during the ice retreat stages. Evidence for this episode of late glacial and post glacial fluviatile activity can be examined in the upper Dovey valley (Itinerary 11).

11. THE DOVEY (DYFI) VALLEY, SN 860125 Late Pleistocene and Holocene sediments and landforms. Figure 30. (M.R.D. & A.P.J.)

This itinerary offers the opportunity to examine landforms and sediments that document the evolution of an upland valley floor. At first glance glaciated valleys, like the Dovey, appear uncomplicated, but in detail they contain complex erosional and depositional histories that encompass supraglacial and subglacial processes, braided and meandering fluvial conditions, ephemeral lacustrine episodes together with valley-marginal deposition such as alluvial fans and screes. The fundamental control throughout the period from the Late Pleistocene to the Present Day is climatic change.

The parabolic, glaciated and infilled Dovey valley can be traced from the Aran mountains in the E to the coastal estuary, with submarine extensions into Cardigan Bay; a distance of more than 48 km. The form and line of the lower valley is tectonically controlled, such that glacial overdeepening has lowered the rockhead in the estuary entrance to -90 m OD. The valley is bordered to the north by the Aran mountains, a ridge of resistant Ordovician volcanic rocks that extend from Cader Idris in the W to the Arenigs in the E. Aran Fawddwy, at 990 m, is the highest point along the ridge and overlooks the source lake of the river (SN 868227). To the S lie less resistant basinal sediments of Ordovician and Silurian age.

The section selected for study extends from Mallwyd to Cemmaes, a distance of 7 km. Use O.S. Sheet 125 Bala & Lake Vyrnwy for this itinerary. Drive to Machynlleth and then E along the A489, join the A470 at Cemmaes Road and travel to Mallwyd. Bridges at both ends of this section link to a

The Aberystwyth District

minor road that runs along the west bank. (Those wishing to examine the
upper valley should drive on to Dinas Mawddwy and turn right on a minor road
that follows the line of the river towards its source). The following landforms
may be observed: hummocky topography, ephemeral lakes, terraces, alluvial
fans and a well developed meandering river channel.

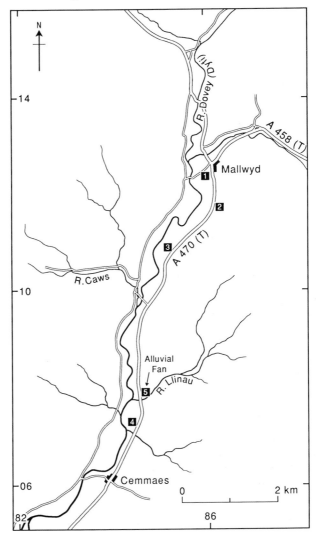

Figure 30: Location map for Itinerary 11, the Dovey (Dyfi) valley.

The Aberystwyth District

Late glacial deposits, mainly seen as hummocky topography with included kettle holes, occur around Mallwyd, but they are difficult to recognise. The hummock landform is the weathered surface expression of glaciofluvial outwash deposits, beneath which lies a melt-out till. Depending on exposure, till, overlain by outwash sediments, can be seen in a section close to the gorge at Mallwyd (**Loc. 1**), (SN858122). Other features, including a group of three well preserved kettle holes (**Loc. 2**) (SN 862122), may be examined close to the roadside. One, with a diameter of 85 m, seen as a shallow boggy depression, contains peat of early Holocene age. These features represent dead ice topography formed during ice wastage and retreat.

Downstream, at Cemmaes Road (SN 824049) (which lies off Figure 30), where the river Twymyn joins the Dovey, an extensive set of cross-bedded sediments overlain by poorly sorted gravels may be examined. Access to this section is at the end of a narrow lane running from the Cemmaes Road roundabout, and through a farmyard (SN 818045). The deposits are considered to represent a delta prograding into a lake during deglaciation of the valley. For a lake to form, an obstruction, probably a cross-valley moraine, is implied. As the valley is 1.2 km wide at this point it is reasonable to assume that the blocking of the valley occurred 2.5 km downstream where the valley narrows to 0.6 km. Water ponding may also have been due to the build-out of flanking alluvial fans. Subsequent reworking of the valley fill by a braided stream system created the erosional unconformity and deposited the overlying gravel in the form of braid bars.

The highest terrace is preserved extensively in the upper valley, but can be examined in the lower reaches. It ranges in height from 6 to 20 m above the present river, has a steep scarp, uneven upper surface and in several reaches is under active erosion by the modern river. This terrace may be examined near **Loc. 1** at Mallwyd where it grades into hummocky topography with associated kettle holes.

The middle terrace is 3 to 8 m above the present river; it appears discontinous as locally it has been eroded back to the scarp of the higher terrace. However, it is always found in association with the highest terrace and may be viewed at Blaenplwyf Uchas (**Loc. 3**). A well preserved section through this terrace is exposed at **Loc. 4**, 500 m downstream of the river Llinau confluence (SN 846075). Here, gravel lenses with crude cross-stratification pass up into horizontally stratified gravel deposits which are overlain by river silts and muds. The sequence is interpreted as having been deposited by a braided stream with incursions of poorly sorted alluvial fan gravels.

The lowest terrace is between 1.5 and 2 m above the present river and, as a consequence, may be confused with the present floodplain. A delimiting scarp edge is rarely seen. All three terraces show traces of earlier fluvial activity in the form of palaeochannels, seen as swampy, sinuous belts often located at the foot of the terrace scarps.

Alluvial fans extend into the valley from both sides. They are of two types: fans associated with the main tributaries and those associated with debris flows sourced from the steep valley sides. The former are extensive (1 km²), with a low surface angle (2°), thickly vegetated, entrenched by streams and are related in time to the sediments that form the highest terrace. The largest tributary related fan is that associated with the river Llinau (**Loc. 5**).

The meanders of the modern river are irregular with swan neck bends, but no cut-offs are evident. Well developed point bars are composed of imbricated gravel clasts. Several point bars are cut through by chutes or storm channels that form when the river is in spate. Mid-channel bars are common.

Thus, the valley records a history of glacial erosion during episodes of ice advance, intermittent ice retreat with melt-out till, push moraines or glaciotectonic till; and reworking of sediment, abandoned at the snout of the glacier, by meltwater streams that were initially proximal to the ice front, but later distal. These events occurred about 15,000 BP and were followed by the disappearance of the ice cap. The rapid climatic amelioration, about 13,000 BP, encouraged vegetation cover and sediment stabilization and hence a decline in sediment supply to the lower valley. Reduced sediment supply, together with glaciosiostatic uplift, encouraged reworking of the valley floor deposits through channel incision, seen today as terracing.

Sediments forming the upper terrace consist of ice-margin lithofacies that are overlain unconformably by outwash sands and gravels. The middle terrace is composed of braided stream deposits, particularly lenses of gravel and cross-bedded sands; whilst the lower terrace is characterised by fining upward sequences that accumulated on point bars in a meandering stream environment, a description that applies to the modern river.

Return to Machynlleth along the A470.

12. TONFANAU. Quaternary erratics and Cardigan Bay geology. Ordovician Vulcanism. Tonfanau Quarry: Volcanics and intrusion. Figure 31. (R.C. & W.T.P.).

Leave the A493 at Rhoslefain c. 2 km south of Llangelynin, park beside the abandoned railway station (SH 564038) near to a line of low sea-cliffs and descend to the shore. A borehole here proved: Quaternary gravel and till, 36.9 m on Tertiary clay, silt sand with some lignite and conglomerate which includes clasts of the underlying rocks, at the base. At 71.1 m these rest upon Cambro-Ordovician grey sandstones and siltstones of nearly vertical dip, seen 4.93 m. The contact between the Tertiary and the Cambro-Ordovican strata dips at 45 degrees and has every appearance of being depositional rather than faulted. The main Tonfanau Fault throwing down Tertiary and Mesozoic strata to the west, lies immediately offshore and it is considered that the borehole

The Aberystwyth District

penetrated a thin veneer of Tertiary strata east of the main fault, as far as the railway at least.

The cliffs expose up to 4 m of till overlain by fluvioglacial yellow clay, sand and gravel (**Loc. 1**) locally in channels (**Loc. 4**). The till is a boulder-rich calcareous sandy clay in which the clasts are mainly less than 50 cm across (**Loc. 6**) though some are as large as 1.5 m. They include Lower Palaeozoic igneous and sedimentary rocks, but the main interest lies in the discovery of many of Jurassic and Tertiary origins. The Jurassic rocks are ironstones and calcareous siltstones yielding pectenid bivalves, ammonites and other fossils, while the Tertiary rocks are poorly lithified silts and clays with lignite. Many erratic boulders have weathered out of the cliffs to remain isolated on the foreshore. They include a large boulder of Jurassic brown calcareous siltstone with belemnites and shells (**Loc. 5**). In some places (**Loc. 2**) the till lacks clasts and is yellow and sandy.

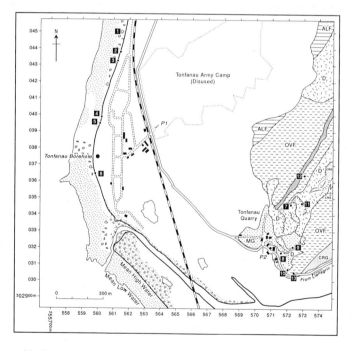

Figure 31: Location map for Itinerary 12, the Tonfanau foreshore and quarry. ALF is the Allt Lwyd Formation, OVF is the Offrwm Volcanic Formation, D is dolerite, CRG is the Cregennen Formation and MG refers to made ground on the western side of the quarry. Much of the area covered by the map is mantled with glacial deposits and has been left blank. (Based on mapping by R. A. B. Bazley, B. G. S.)

The Aberystwyth District

The traditional view of the origin of till on this coast is that it was derived from the hills to the east and was transported by Welsh Ice. However, the till must have plundered the floor of Cardigan Bay to the west of the Tonfanau Fault and it is noteworthy that the till has not yielded Cretaceous flints which are present further south along the coast. Cretaceous rocks are not present on the floor of Cardigan Bay.

Also of interest here is Sarn-y-Bwch, a narrow ridge of boulders and gravel which is emergent at low tide and passes out straight into Cardigan Bay. It is one of three such sarnau, the others being Sarn Badrig 9.5 km SSW of Harlech and Sarn Cynfelyn (58808573) at Wallog, N of Aberystwyth (see Itinerary 6). It has been suggested that these arose as late Devensian median moraines between piedmont glaciers flowing out from the E (Figure 45) although no landward continuations are recognised either at Sarn y Bwych or Sarn Cynfelyn. Another difficulty with the median moraine proposal is the till directly on the landfall of Sarn-y-Bwch (**Loc. 6**) contains boulders of ironstone with Jurassic fossils, whereas a piedmont glacier from the Mawddach estuary area would have transported only Lower Palaeozoic detritus. It is conceivable that Tertiary rocks could have been entrained from the area west of the Mochras Fault and northeast of Tonfanau, but there are no Jurassic rocks subcropping there. It is possible that the sarn is of mixed origin with material derived from the Irish Sea Ice, or that the Jurassic blocks are a legacy of pre-Devensian ice activity. Examine the suggested ice flow patterns shown in Figure 45 together with the geological map of Cardigan Bay (Figure 48) and make your own assessment. Return to the railway station.

Ordovician Vulcanism

In the Lower Palaeozoic the Welsh Basin was part of the northern margin of Eastern Avalonia, itself a small part of the northern edge of continental Gondwana. To the north lay the Iapetus Ocean situated over oceanic crust, beyond was continental Laurentia. During the Lower Palaeozoic the two continents were convergent and for most of the Ordovician this convergence was facilitated partly by the southward subduction of Iapetus oceanic crust beneath Eastern Avalonia. This subduction is believed to have started in late Tremadoc times and in Wales it initiated a cycle of Ordovician vulcanism which commenced with the eruption of the basaltic Rhobell Volcanic Group near Dolgellau and the Trefgarne Volcanic Group in Pembrokeshire. Both are the products of island-arc vulcanism. Subsequent Ordovician vulcanism (Arenig-mid-Caradoc inclusive) was of a back-arc environment, the island-arc having migrated northwards beyond Wales. It is recorded in the spectacular mountainous terrain of North Wales and produced the Aran Volcanic Group seen in Cader Idris.

In late Caradoc times the southward subduction ceased as did the back-arc vulcanism. The next part of Itinerary 12 examines tuffs of the early part of this back-arc vulcanism and Itinerary 13 is devoted to the tuffs of its finale. The igneous intrusions are coeval with the volcanic rocks; they are petrographically similar and do not affect formations younger that the Aran Volcanic Group. Thus the Tonfanau dolerite (Itinerary 12) is probably related directly to one of the basic phases of the Aran Volcanic Group.

Tonfanau Quarry

Proceed by foot or car from the railway station to Tonfanau Quarry (SH 57050320) about 1.25 km away. This is a working quarry and entry requires permission. Here, a large mass of basic magma was intruded into the Offrwm Volcanic Formation, of Arenig and Llanvirn age, to form a sill-like body of dolerite, mainly concordant, but with uneven margins and apophyses, some discordant and others concordant, into the country rocks. One major discordant element extends northwards from the main quarry area, where it intrudes into lower parts of the Offrwm Volcanic Formation and this might have been the feeder to the sill. Large rafts (< 10 m x 15 m) of tuff are aligned parallel to the margins of the intrusion (**Loc. 7**). The dolerite is a multiple intrusion and thus exhibits a number of facies of different grain-sizes. The initial intrusion is a dolerite of medium grain-size which can be examined at **Loc. 8**, immediately east of the road and south of the main quarry. Nearby, the upper contact of the dolerite is visible at **Loc. 9** and **Loc. 10**; the latter has a dip of 70 degrees towards 312 degrees. The later intrusion forms a stockwork of fine-grained dolerite within the early intrusion. The margins of this were chilled against the host dolerite and thus consist of a selvage, some 10 mm thick, of very fine-grained rock. These facies are visible in the highest gallery of the quarry at **Loc. 11**.

Petrographically, the Tonfanau dolerite is similar to others in the district. It is non-porphyritic with subophitic and/or equigranular textures. There is a groundmass of interlocking crystals of zoned albite/oligoclase, probably albitised calcic plagioclase and interstitial chlorite with ophitic plates less than 10 mm across of black titaniferous augite. The chilled margins are locally vesicular and have phenocrysts of feldspar in a groundmass of microlites and chlorite.

The Offrwn Volcanic Formation, which hosts the doleritic intrusion, consists of acidic tuffs, thin tuffites and mudstone. Here the main element is acidic tuff in sequences less than 80 m thick separated by mudstone. The formation records the first volcanic outburst of the Aran Volcanic Group.

At **Loc. 12** mudstone has yielded the graptolite *Didymograptus (D) artus*? indicating the *artus* Biozone of the Llanvirn Series. The tuffs are the product of violent eruptions (nuées ardentes) following the uplift and possible emergence from the sea of the area to the northeast, around Cader Idris. At Tonfanau, however, the graptolitic mudstone intercalations prove that deposition was submarine and the absence of shallow water sedimentary structures suggests emplacement at some depth. Regionally, the tuffs thicken westward, suggesting a volcano lay where Cardigan Bay now is. These tuffs are exposed in a small quarry (**Loc. 13**)

The Aberystwyth District

(SH57230304) beside the cattle-grid on the road from Llanegryn. They are very siliceous and with the aid of a hand lens crystals of quartz up to 2 mm long are visible.

13. BIRD ROCK, SH 64360686 and CASTELL Y BERE, SH 66770856.

Ordovician (Caradoc) vulcanism. Figures 32 and 33. (R.C. & W.T.P.).

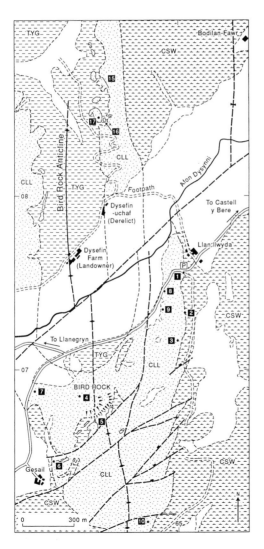

a) Ash flow tuffs.
Follow the A 493 coast road from Tywyn northwards towards Llanegryn (SH 602056), then travel northeastward along the unclassified road for 5.3 km to a parking place P (Figure 32) (SH 65000758), 100 m S of the farm Llanllwyda. The road from Abergynolwyn (SH 678069) is suitable for cars only.

Figure 32: Location map for Itinerary 13. CSW is the Ceiswyn Formation, CLL the Craig Cau Formation and TYG is the Ty'r Gawen Mudstone Formation. The Bird Rock Anticline and the Bodilan Fawr Syncline are indicated. Bold dashed lines are faults, light dashed lines are inferred formation boundaries. Blank areas are glacial and Recent sediments.

The Aberystwyth District

Bird Rock (Craig yr Aderyn) is an imposing hill rising abruptly from the southern margin of the silted-up Dysynni estuary. It comprises an acidic ash-flow tuff *c*. 100 m thick and its overburden, *c*. 5 m thick, of thinly bedded fine-grained acid tuffs and more thickly bedded tuffites with very thin partings of mudstone, all of the Craig Cau Formation.

The Craig Cau Formation is a constituent of the uppermost of three groups of such Ordovician formations, of which the Offrwm Volcanic Formation forms the lowest at Tonfanau. Mudstones separate these groups of formations and eastwards they become thinner until east of Cader Idris the lower part of the Ordovician is dominantly volcanic rocks. Thus this Arenig to Caradoc sequence has been called the Aran Volcanic Group.

The Craig Cau Formation has a thickness in the east of *c*. 400 m, but west of Castell y Bere it is thinner, so that near Bryn-crug SW of Bird Rock the formation is absent. In Bird Rock it occupies a sharp N-S trending anticlinal structure which at its south end plunges southward carrying the tuffs down beneath mudstones of the Ceiswyn Formation. The anticlinal form is best seen from a distance of several hundred metres, or more.

The ash-flow tuff is massive, green on freshly fractured surfaces, but after prolonged weathering it develops a white skin. In contrast with the older tuffs at Tonfanau, most crystals are of feldspar rather than quartz, but otherwise the appearances are similar and difficult to distinguish from rhyolite. There is much silification, quartz veining and numerous small silica nodules.

In thin section many glass shards (or pumice fragments) are visible. These were the walls of exploding gas bubbles within the erupting magma and in places a contorted welded fabric is present proving that the ash-flow was still very hot when emplaced despite the submarine environment. The magma might have released some lava into the sequence, for example the rhyolite at Castell y Bere.

The thinly bedded tuffs which overlie the ash-flow tuff are perhaps comparable with similar deposits above other mass-flow deposits, such as the Volcanic Conglomerate at Montgomery. It is suggested that these are the aftermaths of mass-flow, the products of aqueous turbidity currents caused by subsequent minor instabilities of the proximal areas of the flow. The base of the formation is equally interesting, for in many places it was the locus of soft-sediment disruption, caused when the dense ash-flow was loaded suddenly upon a sea-floor of less dense wet mud. Basal parts of the tuff became detached and foundered into the soft substrate. Now they are visible as pods of tuff surrounded by mudstone of the Ty'r Gawen Mudstone Formation. In this respect there is a close resemblance to the Capel Curig Tuff of northern Snowdonia.

The Aberystwyth District

b) Ash-flow tuffs and soft sediment disruption.
From the parking place ('P' Figure 32) a footpath leads southward affording access to the eastern side of Bird Rock. By the side of the path close to the parking place 4.5 m of bedded acid tuffs and tuffites at the top of the Craig Cau Formation are exposed (SH 64980757) (**Loc. 1**). These are overlain by mudstones of the Ceiswyn Formation. This contact between tuffs and mudstones can be followed southwards in exposures (**Loc. 2**) on the side of the rocky ridge west of the path. Slightly higher, acid tuffs are visible, engulfed within the top 10 m of the ash-flow tuff (**Loc. 3**).

500 m from **Loc. 2** a branch of the path leads west-southwestwards towards the summit via a minor col (SH 64940697). Here, more bedded tuffs are exposed dipping 77 degrees SE. The area of the summit itself (**Loc. 4**) provides good exposures of the main part of the ash-flow tuff. It also provides a fine view of the silted-up Dysynni Estuary. This was probably tidal to the foot of the Rock about 6,000 years ago in post-glacial times. The present river is canalised, but in low light the meandering traces of former courses are clearly visible on the alluvial flats. The precipitous north face of the Rock is dangerous and should be avoided. It is also a nesting site for cormorants and care should be taken not to disturb the birds during the nesting season. The quarry beneath this north face is also very dangerous and should be viewed from the road. Quarrying has stripped off part of the extensive scree deposits revealing Ty'r Gawen Mudstone, with nearly horizontal bedding, beneath the ash-flow tuff in the core of the Bird Rock Anticline.

On the way down welded ash-flow tuff can be examined in several exposures e.g. **Loc. 6**, by a wall 100 m NE of Gesail; **Loc. 7**, 10 m E of the road side; **Loc. 8**, at the roadside and nearby **Loc. 9**, just above the scree; or **Loc. 10** on the S side of Bird Rock, 180 m WSW of Bwlch-y-maen. However, before commencing the main descent, the area c. 100 m S of the Iron Age fort, **Loc. 5**, should be examined. It lies in the core of the anticline and exposes the base of the Craig Cau Formation where the ash-flow tuff has foundered into wet muds of the Ty'r Gawen Mudstone Formation. The resultant formational boundary is complex and large pods of tuff, up to 40 m long, are surrounded by mudstone. The disruption is bounded on the south by a fault which, one may speculate, was of syn-depositional origin.

A less strenuous examination of much more of the formation can be made at the old Welsh castle of Castell y Bere (SH 66770856) (Figure 33). Here the bedded tuffs at the top of the formation are responsible for the prominent dip-slope southeastwards from the castle and they can be examined, (**Loc. 11**) along the path at its base. In the sequence close by, **Loc. 12**, due S of the corner of the castle, is a flow-banded rhyolite (acid lava). The subjacent acid ash-flow tuff is exposed around and to the NW of the castle, and within the castle (**Loc. 14**), 'rafts' of laminated tuff up to 2.0 m long are enveloped by it.

The Aberystwyth District

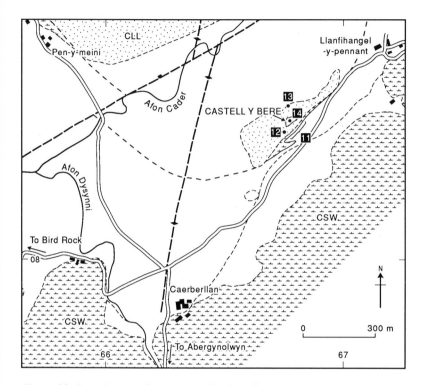

*Figure 33: Location map for itinerary 13, Castell y Bere section. CSW is the
Ceiswyn Formation, and CLL the Craig Cau Formation. Blank
areas are glacial and Recent sediments.*

For anyone with an interest specifically in the sedimentary loading and
disruption at the base of the Craig Cau Formation this aspect is displayed
well in the flanks of the Bird Rock Anticline north of the Dysynni Valley
(Figure 32), particularly in the eastern limb where the formation thins
northward to become absent in places. A track north of Dysefin-uchaf (SH
64530792) crosses and recrosses the base of the formation which here also
includes some lapilli tuff (SH 64600852), autobrecciated rhyolite (SH
64650801), green porphyritic rhyolite (SH 64530869) and 'disturbed'
mudstones. North of the track (SH 64550834) large lobes of massive tuff at
the base of the formation penetrate into the subjacent Ty'r Gowen
Formation **(Loc. 15)**. As at Bird Rock many of the lobes are detached and
form large ellipsoids e.g. at **Loc. 16** 10 m x 5 m; **Loc. 17** 80 m x 50 m and
Loc. 15 50 m x 30 m of nodular tuff (Figure 32).

The Aberystwyth District

14. LLWYNGWRIL, SH 59941107. Cambrian stratigraphy, igneous intrusions and minerals. Figures. 34 and 35. (R.C. & W.T.P.).

A lay-by (SH 60051110) at the side of the main A493 just N of Llwyngwril will accommodate vehicles up to coach size and can be approached from the N (via Dolgellau) or the S (via Tywyn). From this lay-by, marked P on Figure 34 walk SW for *c.* 350 m along the main A493 road then turn W into a narrow footpath down to the beach. From there proceed NE towards the mouth of the river Caletwr (SH 59941107). Excellent exposure reveals a sequence of middle Cambrian strata; first the manganiferous mudstones of the upper part of the Gamlan Formation, then the overlying Clogau Formation of black mudstones with thick turbiditic sandstones, and finally the Maentwrog Formation of thinly interbedded mudstones and sandstones. Trilobites (Paradoxididae) occur, but extraction is difficult.

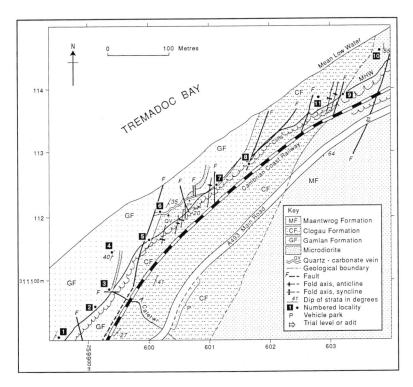

Figure 34: Location map for Itinerary 14, Llwyngwril.

The Aberystwyth District

Stratigraphy of the Cader Idris area

O R D	Rhobell Volcanic Group	
------		Dol-cyn-afon Fm. (Mudstones)
C		Dolgellau Fm. (Black mudstones)
A	Mawddach Group	Ffestiniog Flags Fm. (Siltstones)
M		Maentwrog Fm. (Turbiditic Sst.)
B		Clogau Fm. (Hemipelagites)
R I		
A N	Harlech Grits Group	Gamlan Fm. (Mn mudstones)

The first exposure and the lowest horizons to be encountered (**Loc. 1**) are 116 m SW of the mouth of the river Caletwr. They consist of beds, 0.2 - 0.5 m thick, of pale grey and green mudstone with widely spaced, weakly graded siltstones up to 10 m thick. The muds were largely homogenised by burrowing animals and, somewhat later, cubes of pyrite developed which are scattered throughout (**Loc. 2**); also common are small, green reduction spots. The siltstones display ripple cross stratification and both planar and convolute lamination.

At the mouth of the river (**Loc. 3**) is a dyke of microdiorite trending approximately NNE-SSW. It is up to 2.5 m thick, but pinches out northwards and is cut off southwards by a small fault. It is likely that this was intruded into the Gamlan Formation as a feeder to the volcanoes of Ordovician age (see Itinerary 12).

The upper part of the Gamlan Formation contains many small concretions each comprising a shell of manganiferous garnet and quartz. They have diameters of generally less than 10 mm and in form vary from ellipsoidal to tubular and U-shaped. They may well have nucleated on the benthic burrows present. The manganese content of the rocks is attested by the purple weathering stains to be seen on cliffs between localities 1 and 2.

Towards the top of the formation (**Loc. 4**), fine sandstones < 8 cm thick and siltstones, pale green in colour, become common and purple and green stripes are present in the mudstones. It will be noted that the stripes are not all concordant and thus must be of secondary, diagenetic origin. One metre below the base of the overlying Clogau Formation is a layer of prominent cone-in-cone concretions up to 0.6 m long and up to 0.1 m thick. At **Loc. 5** the dip carries them down northwards to the base of the cliff.

Close by, on the foreshore (**Loc. 6**), a nearly bedding-parallel composite vein of quartz and carbonate separates the Gamlan Formation from the Clogau

The Aberystwyth District

Formation. This can be traced northeastward into the base of the cliffs, where it terminates against a N-S fault (**Loc. 7**).

On the wave-cut platform is a second igneous intrusion. Like the dyke it is composed of microdiorite, but unlike the dyke it is concordant with the bedding and thus a sill *c.* 20 m thick and truncated by the quartz-carbonate vein.

Low-density, mud-rich turbidity currents were mainly responsible for the Gamlan Formation and the absence of shallow water sedimentary structures implies deposition beneath wave base. Nevertheless, trilobites in the equivalent strata on St. Tudwal's Peninsula show little evidence of transportation and Crimes (1970) concluded, therefore, that the water was not deep. Intensive burrowing was caused by a healthy infauna and indicates a well oxygenated sea-floor.

The Clogau Formation in total comprises *c.* 80 m of turbiditic mudstone, siltstone and sandstone. There are 5 intervals, up to 8 m thick, in which the mudstone is characterised by layers of black, laminated hemipelagite containing an abundance of pyrite framboids. It is a much less colourful formation than the Gamlan, but it is the formation that, elsewhere around the Harlech Dome, is veined by auriferous quartz. Indeed, small exploration levels for gold were made in this coastal section too (**Loc. 8**).

The lowest beds of the formation are exposed in the cliffs (SH 60001114) *c.* 80 m NE of the river Caletwr and just E of **Loc. 5**. They are present northeastward for *c.* 200 m to a quartz veined fault (**Loc. 8**), (SH 60171128) on which there is a trial level. Most of this cliff section is depicted in Figure 35, where the measurements were made skirting the foot of the cliffs.

The basal 1.5. m - 2.0 m of beds constitute a transition from the Gamlan Formation and comprise alternations of bioturbated silty mudstone with manganiferous nodules, typical of the Gamlan, and black laminated mudstone with interbeds of turbiditic mudstone and siltstone heralding the Clogau. These are superseded first by 4 m of thinly bedded black mudstone and silty mudstones with laterally impersistent sandstones up to 0.6 m thick, then by 10 m of thinly and thickly bedded quartzose sandstones. Near the top of the formation several soft, green mudstone layers up to 10 cm thick are probably metabentonites formed as deposits of fine dust from distant explosive volcanic eruptions. Intervals of mudstone rich in black phosphatic concretions also appear near the top of the formation and while the laminated hemipelagites, which appear in parts throughout the formation, indicate anoxic conditions of deposition, those parts with phosphatic concretions were deposited under oxygenated conditions (Cave & Hains, 1986). In general the formation indicates a fairly abrupt increase in the energy and density of turbidity currents, and the rapid change from a dominantly oxic basin to one which was anoxic for much of the time.

The Aberystwyth District

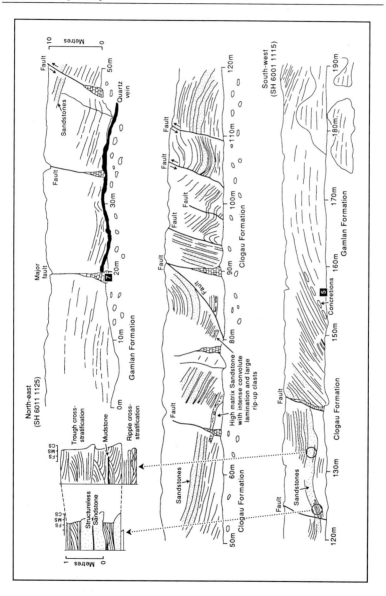

Figure 35: Sketch of the cliffs at the Llwyngwril coastal section. Small scale sedimentary logs illustrate the lateral variation in the sandstones near the base of the Clogau Formation.

The Aberystwyth District

The whole of the succeeding Maentwrog Formation, 540 m thick, is exposed in the cliffs from its base at **Loc. 9** northeastwards towards Fairbourne,but only the basal part is included in this itinerary. The formation conformably overlies the Clogau Formation with the base placed at the appearance of white weathering, well cemented, quartzose and micaceous siltstones and fine sandstones 0.3 cm - 20 cm thick **(Loc. 9)**. These sandstones and siltstones which appear abruptly and in abundance, characterise the formation and can be examined also on the foreshore **(Loc. 10)**. They possess plane-parallel, ripple-cross and convolute lamination and starved ripples are common also. Ripple foresets and sole structures (flute-casts and groove-casts), where they can be found, indicate a northward direction of transportation.

At best macrofossils in these formations are very sparse, but the discovery of the trilobite *Plutonoides (Paradoxides) hicksii* (Salter), on the foreshore **(Loc. 11)** 36 m below the top of the Clogau Formation (SH 60281138) indicates a position in the *Tomagnostus fissus Biozone* of the St. David's Series. Sponge spicules accompanied the trilobite.

The Plynlimon Area (D.E.B.B.)

The rocks of the Plynlimon area (Pumlumon Fawr) comprise a sequence of deep water sedimentary rocks, made famous by the work of O.T. Jones (1909, Jones & Pugh, 1915, 1935) who mapped the area during the first decade of the twentieth century. More recently British Geological Survey mapping by R. Cave and others has led to the publication of the Aberystwyth district sheet (No.163, both solid and drift editions) and accompanying memoir (Cave & Hains 1986). The succession is of Ashgill (Upper Ordovician) and Llandovery (Lower Silurian) age. The sediments are predominently fine grained, consisting of mudstones and shales (many now poorly cleaved slates) and graded siltstones and sandstones, with the occasional development of coarse sandstones. Based on the work of the BGS the general succession in the Plynlimon - Ponterwyd district is as follows:

	metres
Llandovery Series	
Devil's Bridge Formation	300-600
Cwmsymlog Formation	0-140
Derwenlas Formation	20-100
Cwmere Formation	70-145
Ashgill Series	
Brynglas Formation	100-200
Drosgol Formation	370-400
Nant-y-moch Formation	290

Cave (1980) and Cave & Hains (1986) have provided a modern interpretation of the sequence as comprising turbiditic and pelagic sediments. The turbiditic

The Aberystwyth District

units are mainly formed of Bouma Tc-e divisions, the pelagic shales and mudstones of dark coloured, anoxically deposited graptolitic sediments, the lighter oxically deposited bioturbated mudstones being without graptolites.

The Nant-y-moch Formation is a rhythmically deposited and thinly-bedded turbidite sequence, predating the late Ashgill Hirnantian glaciation, of couplets of sandstones, siltstones and mudstones. Two subfacies are described by Cave & Hains: The Craig y Dullfran subfacies comprises sandstones and pale oxic bioturbated mudstones, the Maesnant subfacies thin arenites and dark anoxic shales. These two subfacies alternate in the sequence, and enabled Cave & Hains to plot seven informal members on the 1:50,000 map and in the memoir.

In contrast with the undisturbed bedding of the Nant-y-moch Formation, the succeeding Drosgol and Brynglas Formations are described by Cave & Hains as "pelitic synbasinal melanges", mostly of intrabasinal clasts of contemporary arenite (sandstone), unlithified at the time of mixing, in a matrix of irregularly cleaved argillite. The argillite is largely formed of chlorite and sericite, with fragments of sand size and occasional well-rounded pebbles, and irregular masses of sediment, some up to many metres across.

The Drogsol Formation includes about eight sandstones, each with a maximum thickness of 10 m. The Pencerrigtewion Member, forming the uppermost part of the formation, is the most spectacular of the arenites. It comprises poorly and well-bedded graded sandstones, fine sandstones and mudstones and poorly layered to chaotic units (disturbed beds). The type locality for this unit is high on the northern ridge of Plynlimon, but the member is most easily seen in the Carn Owen periclinal inlier, to the west of the reservoir. The member has been interpreted by Cave & Hains as indicating deposition within and lateral to a series of channels, with sediment transport to the WNW.

The Brynglas Formation is a dark grey massive mudstone with an uneven cleavage, containing sporadic rafts of thinly multilayered arenite. It appears to be similar to the Drosgol Formation, but lacking in the coarse sandstones. Both these formations are believed to have been deposited during the late Ordovician glaciation, when sediment may have been introduced more directly to the slope and basin.

The Brynglas Formation is succeeded abruptly by anoxic graptolite shales of the Cwmere Formation, with graptolites of the *Normalograptus persculptus* Biozone appearing 1 m above the base. The top of the formation is regarded by Cave & Hains as being within the *C.cyphus* Biozone, or in some localities within the '*M*'. *triangulatus* Biozone; i.e. it corresponds approximately with the Lower to Middle Llandovery boundary. Thin turbiditic mudstones and fine arenites are characteristic of the Middle Llandovery Derwenlas Formation, which contains

The Aberystwyth District

the biozones between *triangulatus* and *convolutus*. Graptolites are found mainly in thin rusty-weathering units of anoxic shale, such as those in the classic Rheidol Gorge section. The Cwmsymlog Formation, of *sedgwicki* to *guerichi* Biozone age, marks a change in the type of turbiditic sediment, to colour-banded mud-dominated thin turbidite units with the arenites commonly being less that 5 mm thick. Finally within this area, the youngest beds belong to the Devil's Bridge Formation entirely of *guerichi* Biozone age, a sequence of turbidites of Ta-e pattern, mostly lacking the basal divisions.

All these units possess ESE to WNW current directions, both in the major channelised deposits of the Drosgol Formation, and in the turbidite units of the other formations. Small fans are thought to have been fed from channels in a slope just west of the position of the Towy Anticline. This situation contrasts with that in the later Llandovery and the Wenlock, when northerly directed turbidites supplied the Aberystwyth Grits Formation and later turbidite formations to the east.

The whole succession has been folded along NNE-SSW axes into a complex anticlinorium, with a plunge culmination forming the Plynlimon Ordovician inlier. ENE-WSW normal faulting postdated the folding, and associated lead-zinc mineralisation was formerly exploited in numerous mines. The mountains are regarded by most authors as being a dissected plateau, with a largely superimposed river system. In detail, however, strike ridges are common, the ridge of Carn Owen being a particularly good example, and the harder horizons often form prominences on the hillsides. Deep gullies and ravines are formed along parts of the major faults, good examples being the Hafan Fault at Carn Owen Quarry and the Castell Fault just north of Parson's Bridge.

Glacial features are not prominent in comparison with those found further to the north, though there is a mantling of boulder clay over much of the area. The most striking features are the glacial diversions of the River Rheidol in the region just south of Ponterwyd. The localities are arranged in stratigraphical order, to give a reasonably complete coverage of the region.

15a. NANT-Y-MOCH. SN 763864. Figure 36. (D.E.B.B.).

This locality is best approached from Ponterwyd, turning north off the A44 at the east end of the village at SN751812 onto the minor road signposted to Nant-y-moch reservoir. This road follows the eastern slopes of the Rheidol Valley, running just west of the axis of the Plynlimon Dome, and descending through the Ashgill Brynglas and Drosgol formations into the Nant-y-moch Formation. At a cattle grid at SN 763864 turn right to continue north along the eastern side of the Nant-y-moch Reservoir for a further 2 km to the Maesnant stream. (If time is limited, the uppermost member of the formation may be seen in roadside exposures between SN 763864 and the dam.)

The Aberystwyth District

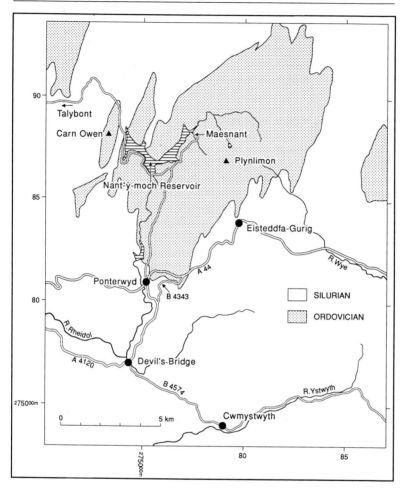

Figure 36: Location map for Itinerary 15 Plynlimon area. The Eaglebrook
mine lies close to the roadside immediately northeast of Carn Owen.

The Maesnant subfacies, forming the lowest member, is exposed some 200
m downstream from the road bridge at SN 77378813, in the periclinal core of
the Plynlimon Dome, and again about 90 m upstream of the bridge, in a higher
member which yields graptolites including *Dicellograptus* cf. *anceps*. The
Craig y Dullfran subfacies (of the second informal member) is well exposed in
the stream on either side of the bridge. Cave & Hains describe bioturbation,
and oversteepened cross bedding with possible water escape structures. Small-
scale folding, with SSW plunges, may also be seen.

The Aberystwyth District

15b. CARN OWEN. Figure 37. (D.E.B.B.).

The uppermost parts of the Ordovician sequence (the Pencerrigtewion Member of the Drosgol Formation, the Brynglas Formation, and the lower part of the Cwmere Formation), together with folding, faulting and mineralisation, are best seen in the Carn Owen Pericline, to the NW of the Nant-y-moch Reservoir.

Follow the road across the Nant-y-moch dam and then NW to **Loc. 1** (SN 73628854), where a track and bridleway join the road. This point can also be reached by following the road E and then S from Talybont, on the A487 N of Aberystwyth. Follow the track SW and then WSW to a small strike ridge (a dip slope) at **Loc. 2** (SN 73368802). The ridge is formed of the basal portion of the Cwmere Formation, containing *Normalograptus persculptus*.

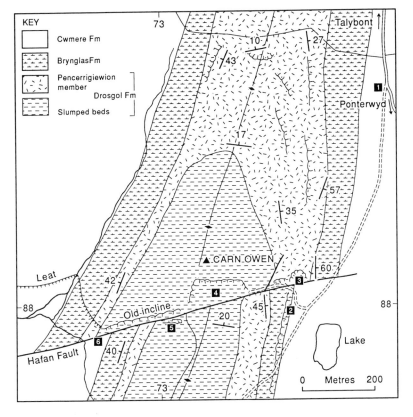

Figure 37: Location map for Itinerary 15b, the Carn Owen area.

The Aberystwyth District

Just north of this ridge, the track leading west to Carn Owen quarry follows a striking topographical depression formed along the Hafan Fault. At the E end the uppermost beds of the Pencerrigtewion Member of the Drosgol Formation are exposed in a small quarry (**Loc. 3**) in which graded sandstones, with an 8 m intercalation of shales, dip steeply to the east. Some beds are lenticular, and loadcasting is strikingly shown, especially on some of the quarried blocks. These sandstones can be traced NNW from here onto the main Carn Owen ridge. About 30 m NE of the quarry an abrupt contact with mudstones of the succeeding Brynglas Formation can be found in a track.

Passing west to the main Carn Owen quarry (**Loc. 4**), and down the succession, the sandstones become massive and unbedded. In this quarry they are underlain by a chaotic unit of disturbed beds, which can justifiably be termed a *melange* and termed Slumped Beds on Figure 37. The quarry face is 150 m wide and over 30 m high, in which are distorted masses of bedded sandstones, up to 20 x 10 m, in a matrix of mudstone. Sandstone dykelets into the mudstones can be found adjacent to the sandstone masses; prominent quartz veins cut the sandstones but not the shales. Mapping of the overall structure shows that the axis of the Carn Owen pericline should pass through the quarry.

Descending the old tramway to the west, similar chaotic beds form the cliff to the north, on the western limb of the pericline (**Loc. 5**). Towards the foot of the incline (**Loc. 6**), they are again succeeded by bedded and graded sandstones similar to those in the small quarry. About 40 m N of the old wheelpit these are in turn succeeded abruptly by mudstones of the Brynglas Formation. It is clear from drawing a cross-section that the bedded sandstones are considerably thinner than on the eastern limb, and that the chaotic beds pass laterally into them.

On the south side of the incline are small adits and opencast workings in the Hafan lode. The worked-out excavations show that the main lodes formed in splays to the main fault, trending in a more easterly direction. Lead, copper and zinc sulphide ores can be collected from the extensive tips (see Itinerary 18 for Eaglebrook mine close by and Cwmystwyth mine).

The Brynglas and Cwmere Formations are both well exposed in this region, on both sides of the fault, and their contacts may be located both in exposures and as changes in topography. Graptolites may be collected from the Cwmere Formation south of the fault at SN 72798790, where a small stream flows north into the main valley, and north of the fault at SN 72768814 where there are old workings in the bank of a south-flowing stream.

If time permits, walk N along the western limb of the main pericline, following the top of the Drosgol Formation to the forestry fence at SN 73158874, and then traverse E across the pericline back to the road via

The Aberystwyth District

Whitestone Quarry (SN 73308870). Only bedded sandstones are exposed; they are whitish weathering, with graded bedding, climbing ripples and loadcast bases. The northward plunge of the pericline can easily be demonstrated here, both by visual inspection of the crags, and by taking a series of strike and dip readings of bedding.

The Carn Owen region can be profitably used as a one or two day mapping area. The boundaries between the Cwmere, Brynglas and Drosgal Formations are easily plotted, and can be used, together with dip and strike measurements, to show that the pericline plunges to the north in the north of the area (it is less easy to demonstrate the plunge in the south, where the closure of the Drosgol/Brynglas boundary is complicated by faulting). Displacement of the units also shows the movement on the Hafan Fault to have been principally vertical. The main difficulty in mapping the area is in following the boundary between the disturbed and bedded sandstones of the Drosgol Formation. For further information on this problem and for an interpretation of the nature of the deposition of the formation, see Cave & Hains (1986).

15c. RHEIDOL GORGE. Figure 38. (D.E.B.B.).

This area makes a convenient half day excursion in itself, but longer if serious fossil collecting is contemplated. If a coach is being used, it can be sent empty from the George Borrow Hotel at Ponterwyd to Ysbyty Cynfyn, where there is ample parking, and the traverse made from north to south. However, if it is not possible to send transport round, then vehicles must be left at one end or the other; geologically and scenically it is more spectacular to start and finish at Ysbyty Cynfyn. The excursion is described, however, as a traverse from N to S.

Follow the farm track which leaves the A44 at the side of the George Borrow Hotel, at the W end of Ponterwyd (SN 74678055). In front of the hotel the River Rheidol flows through a vertical-sided ravine **(Loc. 1)**. This is a glacial diversion (Challinor, 1933); the original valley, now partly exhumed, lying to the E (well seen from the A44 road bridge in Ponterwyd). Follow the track S from the hotel to Bryn-bras farm, and through the farmyard, turn S across a boggy depression and skirt the fields beyond to descend to the Rheidol at **Loc. 2** (SN 75097990).

This was the region described very carefully and fully by Jones (1909). In the traverse alongside the river, the entire sequence is within the Cwmere Formation and the basal portion of the Derwenlas Formation (together making the Rheidol Formation of Jones), spanning the *cyphus* to *argenteus* graptolite biozones of the Lower to Middle Llandovery. A series of crags and cliffs overlooking the river **(Locs. 3 to 4)** are formed of more resistant units within the Derwenlas Formation: the base of these was taken by Jones as the base of his Castell Formation. The main graptolitic horizons are indicated by Jones'

The Aberystwyth District

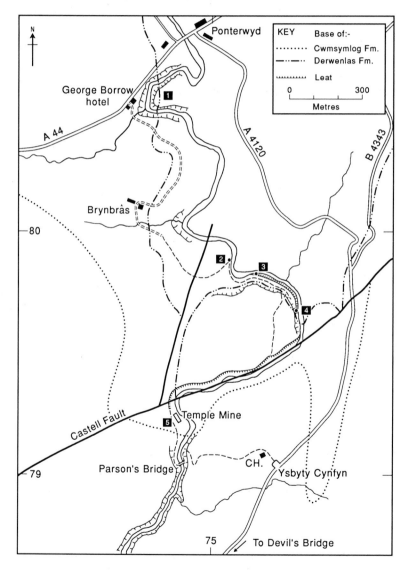

Figure 38: Location map for Itinerary 15c, the Rheidol Gorge.

The Aberystwyth District

locality numbers, and can be found by reference to the upper nodule band, which is taken by Cave & Hains (1986, Figure 32) as the base of the Derwenlas Formation. The two nodule bands form distinctive marker horizons: they weather into small hollows, and the upper horizon has larger nodules, about 30 cm in diameter. The graptolitic horizons are formed of darker and rusty weathering shales, which contrast with the largely unfossiliferous paler strata.

At SN 75097990 (Jones' Locality F12), where the fence bounding the fields leaves the river, the low cliffs are cut in shales of the *A. acinaces* Biozone. *Rhaphidograptus toermquisti* is particularly common.

Follow the river bank downstream, across a scree. This is composed of material from both the Cwmere and Derwenlas Formations, the latter coming from the prominent cliff at the top of the scree. The Cwmere material is rusty weathering cleavage flakes, often yielding graptolites, while the Derwenlas material is of pale flakes, showing graded units about 2 cm thick.

Just beyond the scree an old artificial water course or leat leaves the river to run downstream alongside it. This supplied water to the Temple lead mine further downstream. In the exposures along this leat, particularly at its upstream end, graptolites of the *Coronograptus cyphus* Biozone are common.

Continuous exposures can be followed for the next 300 m downstream, at which point the river plunges down a cascade over the more resistant part of the Derwenlas Formation into a ravine. The leat here was carried in a wooden trough. For the first 200 m this is a strike section, in which variations in dip outline minor folding plunging S. For a further 50 m the path (in reality the old leat) is cut into a low cliff, and finally the river bank widens for the last 50 m before the cascade. Jones' localities F14-18 can be located along this last stretch of bank, as dark rusty weathering horizons contrasting with the pale shades and siltstones.

F14. Top of the Cwmere Formation, 1.9 m below the upper nodule layer: upper part of *cyphus* Biozone.

F15. Derwenlas Formation, 1.9 m above the upper nodule layer: lower part of *triangulatus* Biozone.

F16. 9.1 m above the upper nodule layer: upper part of the *triangulatus* Biozone.

F17. *magnus* band, 11.0 m above the upper nodule layer: *magnus* Biozone.

F18. *leptotheca* band, 19 m above the upper nodule layer: *argenteus* Biozone. This horizon includes the pale "Green Streak", a thin (2 cm) but distinctive shale.

The Aberystwyth District

To continue S to Ysbyty Cynfyn climb up over the scarp formed by the Derwenlas Formation, and follow a narrow path above the ravine. After some 150 m it descends through scrub oak trees to join the leat, which now forms a ledge on the hillside, well above the river level. The river here has excavated its valley along the Castell Fault. Intermittent exposures along the leat are in the Derwenlas Formation. Further SW, the valley and the path turn abruptly S, while the Castell Fault continues its WSW course, along a tributary stream. Just beyond the stream are the ruins of the Temple Mine (**Loc. 5**), which include adits and shafts into the west bank of the Rheidol, a large wheelpit (fed by the leat), and the remains of the processing mill. The tips yield ore and gangue minerals typical of the Cardiganshire ore field.

Follow the path S to Parson's Bridge, and pause to examine the nature of the ravine here, with its gigantic potholes. River flow is normally much less than previously because much of the water is abstracted above Ponterwyd to feed the hydroelectric power station in Cwm Rheidol. Turn over the bridge and then ascend the path to Ysbyty Cynfyn: at first up the steep side of the gorge, and then more gently across the upper valley to the church and road (SN 75307905).

15d. DEVIL'S BRIDGE (PONTARFYNACH). Figure 36. (D.E.B.B.).

Drive S along the A4120 to Devil's Bridge. Note the open nature of the Rheidol Valley here: the gorge is cut as a narrow notch into it, the result of rejuvenation during the Pleistocene. At Devil's Bridge (SN 74157703) the Rheidol turns sharply to the W, and the Mynach, a river graded to the higher open valley of the Rheidol, plunges through a dramatic gorge and down a series of waterfalls to join it. These relationships can be seen both from the terrace opposite the Hafod Arms Hotel and from the bridge itself, while a closer view is possible by passing through the tourist turnstiles.

The Ystwyth Inlier

The aim of this itinerary is to examine the sequence of early to mid-Llandovery (Rhuddanian to Aeronian), predominantly turbiditic rocks, exposed in the core of the southward plunging Teifi Anticlinorium, south of the Ystwyth Fault; a region know geologically as the Ysbyty Ystwyth Inlier. The inlier exposes a sequence of mudstone formations which are punctuated by a series of sandy turbidite facies known collectively as the Ystrad Meurig Grits Formation. The geology of the inlier was mapped by O.T. Jones and more recently by Cave (1979), but this itinerary is largely based on the results of recent BGS mapping and incorporated in the new Llanilar Sheet 178 to which reference should be made.

The Aberystwyth District

16. YSTWYTH AREA. Sandstone lobes, graptolites and Tertiary drainage patterns. Figure 39, BGS Sheet 178 and OS map 135. (J.R.D., R.A.D. & D.W.).

The sandstone turbidite facies of the Ystrad Meurig Grits Formation (Y.M.G.) occur at several discrete levels within the inlier sequence. These levels can be dated using graptolitic horizons both within and between them. Five separate levels of sandstone turbidites are recognised; they are of *acuminatus, magnus-argenteus* early *convolutus,* late *convolutus* and *sedgwickii* Biozone age. Work by the British Geological Survey has established that a link exists between these sandstone sequences and the Caban Conglomerate Formation (C.C.) of the Rhayader area. The C.C. can be viewed in a disused quarry on the Elan valley road (B4518) just west of Rhayader (SN 930650). This is the site of a long lived feeder channel through which sand-rich turbidity currents, sourced from the eastern margin of the Welsh Basin, supplied the various levels of the Y.M.G. 20 km to the west. Based on mapping and dating it would appear that each of these levels represents a separate sand-rich turbidite lobe. Moreover, following lobe abandonment succeeding lobes were located progressively further north.

Travel SE from Aberystwyth along the B4340 to Pont Llanafan (SN 687714); turn left along a minor road towards Pontrhydygroes that runs alongside the river Ystwyth. The river valley follows the line of the Ystwyth fault. Roadside quarries 1.4 km east of the road junction display sandstone turbidites of the Y.M.G. of the early *convolutus* Biozone. Steep, northward facing slickensided rock faces represent an exposed fault plane.

About 3 km E of Pont Llanafan the course of the river Ystwyth is orientated in a more southerly direction off the line of the Ystwyth Fault. Continue across a small bridge over a tributary stream and park by the side of the road. Descend through the woods to view the narrow, spectacularly pot-holed gorge of the river Ystwyth. Rock ledges along the edge of the gorge can be readily examined by small parties proceeding with care. The westward dipping sequence of thin rhythmically interbedded sandstones and mudstone constitutes the type of section of the Chwarel Goch facies, part of the Y.M.G. These strata, of the *acuminatus* Biozone, are the oldest rocks exposed in the Ysbyty Ystwyth inlier and afford an opportunity for large parties or the less agile to examine the rocks of the same age and facies. Sandstone-mudstone couplets (mainly Bouma Tcde), separated by dark grey, laminated hemipelagic mudstones are well seen on the water worn rock faces. The more agile may wish to traverse the sequence downriver. It is possible to see the sandstone units thin gradually, marking their passage from the Chwarel Goch facies to the overlying Cwmere Formation about 50 m upriver from the disused footbridge. Continue E towards Pontrhydygroes and cross the Nant yr Henfelin by the bridge (SN 729718). This tributary of the Ystwyth flows along the course of the proto-river Teifi, a major river system of Tertiary age that drained central Wales. It was at this site that the headwaters of the river Ystwyth, exploiting the fracture zone of the Ystwyth fault belt, captured the upper reaches of the proto-Teifi.

Park in the layby and examine the roadside crags opposite which expose the contact between the Cwmere and Derwenlas Formations. Laminated hemipelagites in the former, that were laid down in stagnant anoxic bottom waters, yield graptolites of the *magnus* Biozone. Bioturbation structures in the Derwenlas Formation mudstones indicate that at the time of deposition bottom conditions were oxic, and soft bodied organisms lived and fed within the sediment.

In Pontrhydygroes turn right and travel along the B4343 to Ysbyty Ystwyth; turn right at the chapel on the minor road to Ystrad Meurig. Pass quarried crags on the left, developed in sandstone turbidites of the Y.M.G. Flute casts indicate sediment transport was from the northeast. Pass Hendre Quarry (but see **Itinerary 17**) and stop near the bend for fine views to the south of Cors Caron, one of the largest raised bogs in Wales. To the E, the broad drift-valley, with its misfit stream the Marchnant, represents the former course of the proto-river Teifi prior to capture of its headwaters in the late Tertiary.

Continue SW to the village of Ystrad Meurig and turn right onto the B4340. A small disused roadside quarry on the western outskirts of the village exposes the upper part of a sequence of sandstone turbidites of the Y.M.G. Lower sections of the quarry expose medium bedded sandstones with parallel, convolute and ripple cross-lamination. These sandstones represent the basal parts of turbidite rhythms consisting of Bouma Tbcde and Tcde. Shallow mudstone draped scours incise and cut out some sandstone beds. The trends of the scours and of the rare flute casts indicate that sediment supply was from the NE. Bundles of thinner bedded sandstones, siltstones and mudstones occur between some of the thicker beds and dominate the higher sequences in the quarry. A packet of beds containing rusty weathering mudstones may by correlated with a similar sequence in Hendre Quarry where laminated hemipelagites have yielded *argenteus* Biozone graptolites.

Return to Ystran Meurig and turn right on a minor road to Swyddffynnon. At Swyddffynnon turn right to Tynygraig and then on to Tynddraeneg Farm located 400 m N of the village on the left of the road. Ask permission at the farm to park vehicles and visit the farm quarry. The quarry exposes the Chwarel Goch facies of the Y.M.G. Graptolites (particularly *Normalograptus parvulus*) are especially common on certain bedding planes.

Proceed N along the minor road to the village of Tynygraig to the disused Tynygraig railway cutting (Figure 39). Exposed in the cutting is a complete

The Aberystwyth District

section through the Aeronian (mid-Llandovery), including the upper part of the Cwmere Formation, the whole of the Derwenlas Formation and the basal part of the Rhayader Mudstones (Cwmsymlog Formation of the Aberystwyth district). Obtain permission at the Tynygraig Post Office to leave vehicles in the parking area opposite. Proceed W along the track that starts to the N of the Post Office, cross the stile and walk to the dismantled railway line. Note the tunnel to the SE is cut in sandstone of the Y.M.G. of *magnus - argenteus* Biozone age. Walk NW along the line of the old track for 700 m passing cuttings in the Derwenlas Formation. The section to be studied extends for 600 m to the NNW.

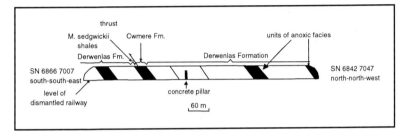

Figure 39: Sketch of the southwest side of Tynygraig railway cutting (disused). Anoxic facies are shown in black.

The W side of the cutting exposes 150 m of oxic facies of the Derwenlas Formation, seen as pale green-grey turbidite mudstones with abundant siltstone laminae interbedded with burrow-mottled hemipelagic mudstones. In the lower half, rusty weathered, dark grey, structureless turbidite mudstones (anoxic facies) alternate with laminated hemipelagic mudstones that contain graptolites of the upper *convolutus* Biozone.

A prominent re-entrant with clay gangue marks the position of a small fault. Anoxic mudstones facies, downthrown to the N, have yielded graptolites of the *sedgwickii* Biozone and are assigned to the *M. sedgwickii* shales, the basal member of the Rhayader Mudstone Formation. Though the rocks of the cutting remain in the anoxic facies for some 30 m NNW of the fault, from a point around 10 m beyond the fault laminated hemipelagites contain graptolites of the older *magnus* Biozone (upper Cwmere Formation). A cryptic zone of fracturing and quartz veining evidently marks the site of a thrust with an effective throw to the S of about 180 m.

Oxic, burrow-mottled mudstones of the Derwenlas Formation overlie the Cwmere Formation in normal succession and make up the bulk of the remainder of the section. Thin anoxic intervals either side of the concrete pillar contain graptolites of the *argenteus* and lower *convolutus* biozones. Two thicker packets of anoxic mudstones in the upper third of the section also yield *convolutus* Biozone graptolites.

It is instructive to note that the cutting, as opposed to the tunnel, fails to display the sandstone facies of the Y.M.G. that are widely developed in the Derwenlas Formation a short distance to the E. The absence of these facies provides an important constraint on the geometry and distribution of these turbidite sand bodies. However, at 160 m, the Derwenlas Formation is significantly thicker than in adjacent areas and this may reflect the greater volume and increased frequency of fine grained turbidity currents on the fringes of the Y.M.G. system.

17. HENDRE QUARRY. A minor lobe of basinal arenaceous turbidites. Figures 40 and 41 and Sheet 178. (R.C.).

Hendre quarry is 19 km SE of Aberystwyth and approached along minor roads from the B4343 at Ysbyty Ystwyth or from the B4340 at Ystrad Meurig. A car park 'P' is situated behind the quarry office at the SW end of the site (Figure 40). It is a working quarry and arrangements for visits should be made with the owners. (Hendre Quarry, Craig y Bwlch, Ystrad Meurig, Pontrhydygroes, Dyfed. Tel 01974 282 606) Hard hats and stout footwear are essential.

The quarry exploits the Ystrad Meuring Grits (Y.M.G.) and the immediately overlying hard, banded silty mudstones to produce a wide range of materials including aggregate, hard-core, tarmacadam, concrete blocks, road dressing and ornamental stone for gardens. The Y.M.G. of Hendre Quarry are part of a lobe, referred to as the Hendre Lobe, of turbiditic sandstones within the mainly mudrocks of the Derwenlas Formation. They are of Aeronian (Middle Llandovery) age. To appreciate both the Llandovery lithostratigraphy and biozonation refer to Appendix 1. This lobe was the earliest of probably three such Aeronian lobes fed through the Caban Canyon near Rhayader (SN 930650). Biostratigraphically it belongs to the *magnus* and *argenteus* Biozones and was spread westward. The later lobes were of *convolutus* and *sedgwickii* Biozone age and spread northwestwards. C.J.N. Fletcher (BGS, 1994) identified the more proximal parts of at least two of these lobes where they are superposed close to their point of divergence near Cwmystwyth. He erected a new formation, the Ystrad Meurig Grits Formation to embrace all these sandstones; thus it is necessary to identify the lobe cropping out around Ystrad Meurig as the Hendre Lobe.

The base of the lobe is diachronous. At Cloddiau (SN721690), the most proximal and central exposure, there are coarse sandstones and granule to pebble conglomerates resting on the anoxic turbiditic and hemipelagic mudstones of the Cwmere Formation. Even under the northern end of Level 5 in borehole 1 the Y.M.G. rest on the Cwmere Formation, but farther north,

The Aberystwyth District

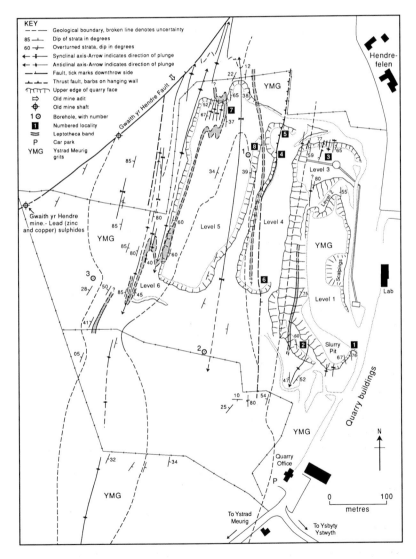

Figure 40: Location map for Itinerary 17, Hendre Quarry.

The Aberystwyth District

Figure 41: Lower photograph shows rhythmically banded silty mudstones medium grey in the lower part. Note the near black phosphatic enriched layers. For further information see last part of Appendix 1. Upper photograph shows flutes preserved on the base of a sandstone; flow is from left to right.

The Aberystwyth District

towards the Ystwyth a bed of medium grey mudstone, typical of the Derwenlas Formation and yielding graptolites of the *triangulatus* and *magnus* Biozones, intervenes between the sandstones and the Cwmere Formation and thickens northwards. A reverse of this condition is believed to exist on the south side of the lobe.

At the top the sandstones thin upwards, fairly abruptly, into dominantly silty mudstones. These are rhythmically banded Bouma Te intervals each being medium grey in the lower part and with dark grey phosphatic enrichment often occurring between the two (Figure 41). Such strata are well displayed at the southeastern side of Level 5 **(Loc. 8)** and represent mud turbidites deposited under oxic basinal water.

Graptolite Bands

The rocks of the Derwenlas Formation are mainly the medium grey distal or slope-apron turbiditic mudstones of an oxic depositional environment, but O.T. Jones observed that they were divided stratigraphically by several thin, dark grey abundantly graptolitic mudstone layers. These graptolite bands resulted from brief changes in the depositional environment from oxic to anoxic and each is named after its characteristic graptolite. Where the basin was invaded by higher energy turbidites, such as the Y.M.G., the dark grey mudstone band has been replaced by a much thicker sequence of sandstones. Nevertheless, when weathered these reveal their deposition under anoxic conditions by their rusty stain and the graptolites present as detritus.

Ystrad Meurig Grits, Hendre Lobe

The lobe consists of layers of greywacke sandstone each embracing one or more of the Bouma, turbidite intervals Ta -Td and, in most parts of the sequence, but not all, separated by silty mudstone of the Bouma Te interval. The thickness of the lobe might be as much as 90 m at its centre; Borehole 3 encountered 58.5 m of sandstones without reaching their base. Borehole 1, on the other hand, proved a total thickness of *c*. 47 m for the sandstone sequence registering a northward thinning compatible with that shown by 1:10,000 mapping. The lobe is tripartite, comprising three cycles. Each cycle commences fairly abruptly with a packet of thick sandstones. Within this packet bed thicknesses are variable, but with an occasional thickening-upwards sequence. Ultimately, the cycle ends with a rapidly fining and thinning-upward passage into a mainly mudstone interval.

Cycle 1

The earliest cycle can be seen at the entrance to the quarry **(Loc. 1)**. The basal beds are obscured under the roadway to the east, but the lowest visible

The Aberystwyth District

are coarse sandstones (grain size greater than 4 mm), commonly structureless and mildly graded Bouma Ta intervals, with parallel laminated Tb intervals in some. Good examples of flute clasts are present on the bases of some beds. Mudstone partings (Bouma Te intervals) are thin or absent. Folds are present in parts of this face, but the thickness of the cycle is probably 40 m. The topmost 5 m can be examined at the SE end of the bench (**Loc. 2**). They occur in the core of an anticline as silty mudstones, with silty laminae, up to 10 cm thick and 26 sandstones 0.5 cm - 3.0 cm thick. Ending the cycle is 10 cm of silty mudstones with silt laminae.

Cycle 2

The second cycle 33.49 m thick, commences abruptly with a 0.8 m bed composed of several sandstones up to 15 cm thick representing Bouma Tab intervals. It records a resurgence in the throughput of the canyon. Two subordinate reactivations of the main cycle are recorded 7.14 m and 10.88 m above the base, by abrupt reappearances of sandstones up to 0.8 m thick. However, overall, the lower part of the cycle consists largely of sandstones of maximum thickness 0.8 m some of which are composite. The upper half of the cycle consists largely of thinly bedded mudstones and sandstones. Near the bottom is a sequence, 1.70 m thick, in which the sandstones thicken upwards from 1 cm to 13 cm terminating in 0.71 m of even thicker sandstones.

Leptotheca Band and Cycle 3

Capping the second cycle are several metres of darker grey, graptolitic, rusty weathering sandstones and mudstones, the *leptotheca* Band of O.T. Jones (1909). The beds cross the western end of the bench at Loc. 2 and pass northward into the high wall of level 1 (Figure 40). A less disrupted exposure (**Loc. 7**) now shows the band is 4.7 m thick. These anoxic strata represent the start of the third cycle. Basinal anoxicity was commonly the result of marine transgression of parts of the basin margin and a marine transgression, albeit brief, tended to curtail the feed of the detritus to the canyon head. Consequently, the thick sandstones, usually expected at the base of a new cycle, appear only when the sequence becomes oxic again. The best exposure of the sandstones of Cycle 3 and the *leptotheca* Band is at **Loc. 7** consisting of beds of sandstone up to 20 cm thick and dark grey mudstone partings of 4 - 20 cm; both have rust-brown stains. Graptolites are present in the sandstones as well as the mudstones. Sole structures, such as flute-casts (Figures 41) and tool marks (groove-casts and prod marks) are present on sandstone bases, but trace-fossils, common on oxic sandstones, are absent. Crystals of quartz, with hexagonal prisms and pyramids can be found here too, derived from irregular small quartz, veins in the steeply dipping strata. Flute-casts are a means by which the flow of palaeocurrents may be assessed. Most of the remainder of the third cycle can be examined in the overlying sandstones sequences as far as the centre of the syncline.

The Aberystwyth District

Folds

The trend of the folds in the quarry is NNE-SSW to N-S in keeping with the regional pattern, but some folds verge westwards, others eastward. One anticline has been seen (**Loc. 2**) and others occur at the northern ends of the levels 3 (**Loc. 3**), 4 (**Loc. 5**) and 7 (**Loc. 7**). A larger syncline traverses the length of level 7. All these folds are affected by a culmination in plunge which lies E-W across northern parts of the quarry.

Faults

Several small, high-angle faults are visible in quarry faces (**Loc. 3**), but the fault of greatest significance is the eastward directed thrust in level 4. It has raised the YMG in its hanging wall to exploitable levels thus making the quarry more viable. A good exposure is that at **Loc. 4** where a sharp hanging-wall anticline in massive sandstones is separated from the banded mudstones of the footwall by a quartz vein several centimetres thick. The vein lies along the thrust-plane and dips westward at about 50 degrees. In the immediately underlying mudstones regularly spaced quartz-filled tension gashes rise up into the thrust plane. These were opened up by drag as the sandstones overrode the mudstones and were synchronously occupied by silica-rich pore fluid.

At **Loc. 5** the hanging wall anticline is accompanied by a syncline, but when traced to the south end of level 4 (**Loc. 6**) the thrust has translated into a plexus of high-angle reverse faults. It appears that in this southward direction the upthrow of the thrust diminishes, compensated by the steep southward plunge of the adjacent syncline. The thrust was proved in Borehole 1 at a depth of 48 m beneath 47 m of sandstones and 1 m of dark grey turbiditic and hemipelagic mudstones of the Cwmere Formation. Examination of the mudstones of the footwall at **Loc. 5** reveals that they dip westward, like the thrust plane, but by means of their banding (see Appendix 1) it can be determined that the beds are inverted as part of the western limb of an easterly verging footwall syncline. A second thrust, associated with tight and ruptured folds in sandstones on level 3 (**Loc. 3**), bounds this syncline on the east. This thrust dips steeply eastwards, opposing the main thrust, and thus the synclinal mudstones form the footwalls of both.

18. CWMYSTWYTH AND EAGLEBROOK MINES. Minerals and mineralisation. Figure 36. (D.E.B.B. & M.R.D.).

Mineralisation in mid-Wales occurred along ENE-WSW trending normal faults and breccia zones that cut across folds of early Devonian age. The normal faults, most commonly, dip S at 55 degrees with downthrows in excess of 150 m and have 10 to 30 m wide, laterally impersistent, breccia zones. Dating suggests that the mineralisation occurred in the Upper Palaeozoic. According

The Aberystwyth District

to Phillips (1970), mineralisation was related to the migration of hydrothermal solutions under conditions of high pressure. Fluid pressure built up until it exceeded the tensile strength of the country rock in the vicinity of a fault plane that acted as the principal conduit. A hydraulic tension fracture resulted with a concomitant drop in fluid pressure that in turn led to mineral precipitation. Mineral zoning in the breccia zone is probably a function of the change in pressure-temperature and solution chemistry. Permeation of the hot solutions into the surrounding rock also promoted mineral crystallisation.

Drive east to Cwmystwyth via the B4574 SE from Devil's Bridge. The road passes through an arch, erected for the Jubilee of George III, at the watershed dividing the Mynach and Ystwyth catchment areas. The Cwmystwyth mines lie 1.5 km E of the village, and this section of the road is narrow, but passable by coach, which can be turned and parked at the mines. It is also possible to take a full-sized coach over the mountain road from Rhayader, although this route is best avoided in summer when there is likely to be too much traffic on the route, which is poorly provided with passing places. Use care during spring as the region is an important nesting area.

At the mines the main Cwmystwyth Fault passes along the main valley, and most of the old workings are in the hillside to the north of the fault. The fault itself is a conspicuous and major feature of the landscape, whether viewed from the ground or from a satellite (as in the BGS satellite view of Wales). The mineralisation occurs in ENE trending lodes emplaced in the Upper Llandovery Cwmystwyth Grits, disposed in a N-S trending syncline, whose axis lies E of the main opencast (BGS 1:50,000 Llanilar sheet).

Look N from the road, to the skyline. A stream can be seen here, plunging down a ravine in a series of cascades past the upper opencast workings and lower spoil tips. Ascend the hillside towards the ravine, eventually reaching a level path. From this point the exposure of some of the lodes can be seen in the opposite river bank. The path eventually peters out, at a point where there was formerly a small bridge across the stream. Scamble across at this point and ascend to the opencast. In this opencast, which is somewhat dangerous, are the exposures of two brecciated fault zones. In these the sequence of mineralisation can be studied.

Abundant minerals (galena and sphalerite) can be collected from the extensive tips, on both sides of the road. The lowest tips are adjacent to the River Ystwyth, and leachates can be observed entering the river both from the tips, and from a low level adit which drains much of the extensive levels.

For those especially interested in minerals the Eaglebrook mine (SN 736892) can also be visited.

Drive N from Aberystwyth on the A487 to Talybont; at the village green take the right fork and another right fork 300 m further on, then the mountain

The Aberystwyth District

road to Nant-y-Moch dam by way of Bryn Mawr. The road runs up the south side of a spectacular glaciated valley with a narrow spillway or meltwater channel at the top. The Eaglebrook mine is on the right hand side of the road 600 m beyond Llyn Nantycagl and before the damned lake is reached.

Eaglebrook mine, also know as Nantycagel, is a site of Special Scientific Interest. The principal mineralisation involves lead and zinc, but copper, nickel and antimony are also present. More than 20 different minerals are known to occur, although the crystals are tiny and associated with gossan. Gossan is the leached and oxidised near-surface part of a vein or lode; hence hydrated iron oxides are usually associated with small quartz crystals. Therefore, to recognise many of the rarer minerals a x 10 hand lens is essential. The following minerals are present: galena, sphalerite, chalcopyrite, malachite, marcasite, native copper, pyromorphite, cerussite, dolomite, quartz and linarite. Most of these minerals are on display in the entrance to the Geology section of the University of Wales, Aberystwyth .

Continue round the lake and across the dam (a gravity buttress type) and on to the village of Ponterwyd.

19. CWMYSTWYTH AREA. Silurian stratigraphy, high matrix turbidites. Figure 42. (J.R.D., R.A.W. R.D.W.).

The village of Cwmystwyth (SN 789741) off the B4574 is a convenient starting point for this itinerary. Proceed E along the Rhayader mountain road for 1.5 km to the site of the abandoned Cwmystwyth mine (for minerals see Itinerary 18). Continue E along road and note Craig Ddu a nivation cirque (SN 811739) to the S. It is floored by periglacial deposits in the form of a soliflucted fan. Further E lies Cwm Tinwen (SN 831748), another cirque with a prominent moraine-like rampart that formed by the glissading of frost-shattered debris down a snow slope.

Beyond the bridge at Blaenycwm, the valley of the river Ystwyth offers unbroken exposure through the upper Cwmystwyth Grits Group that forms part of the western limb of the Central Wales Syncline. Here, the Group reaches its greatest thickness and all the component formations can be examined. Drive to the E end of the valley and leave vehicles at the car park (SN85407582).

Return on foot back along the road for *c.* 1.5. km to the first fence line of the right (SN 83777529) and follow this to the river. From **Loc. 1** to **Loc. 2** there is near continuous exposure of the uppermost Rhuddnant Grits. Here, the sandstone turbidites are of two distinct types: medium to coarse-grained high matrix (argillaceous), commonly graded in beds up to 2 m thick and in bundles up to 15 m thick, and low-matrix quartz-rich in beds less than 5 cm thick and interbedded with mudstones. The high-matrix sandstones probably accumulated from mud-rich turbidity currents or muddy debris flows. Large rope-like groove

The Aberystwyth District

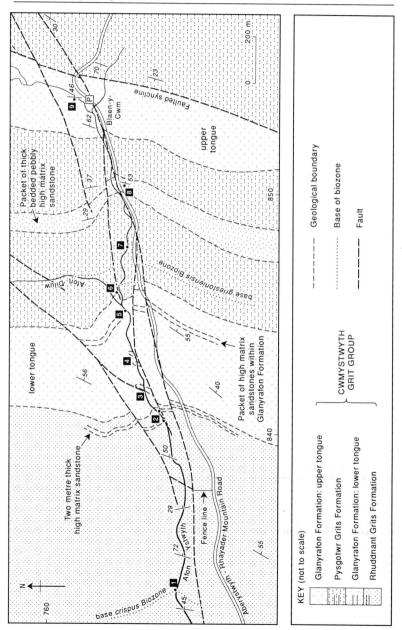

Figure 42: Location map for Itinerary 19, Cwmystwyth area.

The Aberystwyth District

casts could be tectonically modified load features. Unequivocal sole structures confirm a southern derivation. These sandstones may represent delta-fed turbidite lobes; aggradation or lobe buildup promoted abandonment with subsequent flows deflected into adjacent topographic lows on the sea floor. The low-matrix thin-bedded turbidites may have been sourced from a wide area of shelf following storm activity. They would have blanketed the abandoned lobes. Topographic buildup, due to lobe aggradation, induces switching of sites of accumulation, a process that creates compensation cycles. Background sedimentation is seen as laminated hemipelagites; these have yielded *crispus* Biozone graptolites.

Further E at **Loc. 2** (SN 84107550) a 2 m thick high-matrix amalgamated sandstone is displaced by a fault orientated along the river valley. Rope-like sole structures are present on the base of this bed which represents two or more mass-flow events. A short distance upstream interbedded thin turbidite sandstones and mudstones, free of high-matrix sandstones, represent the succeeding Glanyrafon Formation.

The high-matrix sandstones of the Rhuddnant Grits are brought to the surface 100 m upstream in a faulted anticline and again in two further anticlines (**Locs. 3, 4,** and **5**) developed near an old dam (SN 84327560). Upstream, beyond the dam, the river valley provides excellent exposures of the Glanyrafon Formation seen as rhythmically interbedded turbidites and hemipelagites. The basal beds of the succeeding Pysgotwr Grits are exposed immediately upstream of the confluence of the Ystwyth with the Diluw (**Loc. 6**). Graptolites recovered from this site are of the *crispus* Biozone. The sequence is dominated by high-matrix sandstones. 200 m above the base of the Pysgotwr Grits interbedded thin sandstones and mudstones exposed in the core of an anticline have yielded *griestoniensis* Biozone taxa (**Loc. 7**). The acme of deposition of the Pysgotwr Grits is marked by the appearance of thick coarse grained (locally conglomeratic), feldspathic, high-matrix sandstones. These form prominent crags along the N side of the valley and may be conveniently examined along a track 25 m S of the road where amalgamated beds over 3 m thick are exposed (**Loc. 8**).

Walk E to the car park and cross the wooden footbridge to observe thinly interbedded green turbidite sandstones and mudstones of the Glanyrafon Formation of the *griestoniensis* Biozone (**Loc. 9**). Note that the sandstone crags across the valley display a westerly dip; these form part of the eastern limb of the Central Wales Syncline. Return to the road and walk 200 m E for views of the Elan Valley Bog (SN 857754) developed at the watershed between the Elan and Ystwyth drainage systems. Boreholes record a sequence of lacustrine clays overlain by 5 m of peat. Pollen analysis indicated that the lake clays are late glacial and that the peat, which contains birch and juniper, has accumulated since the early Holocene (*c*. 10,000 BP).

The Aberystwyth District

RECOMMENDED FURTHER READING

ADAMS, T.D. 1961. Buried valleys of the Upper Rheidol (Cardiganshire). *Geol. Mag*, **98**, 406-408.

BRITISH GEOLOGICAL SURVEY. 1984. England and Wales Sheet 163: Aberystwyth (Solid).

BRITISH GEOLOGICAL SURVEY. 1984. England and Wales Sheet 163: Aberystwyth (Drift).

CAVE, R. 1980. Sedimentary environments of the basinal Llandovery of mid-Wales. *In* Harris, A.L., Holland, C.H. & Leake, B.E. (eds.) The Caledonides of the British Isles - reviewed. *Spec. Pubs. geol. Soc. Lond.*, **8**, 517-526.

CAVE, R & HAINS, B.A. 1986. Geology of the country between Aberystwyth and Machynlleth. *Mem. Brit. Geol. Surv Sheet 163*, i-ix, 148 pp.

CHALLINOR, J. 1933. The 'incised meanders' near Ponterwyd. *Geol. Mag.*, **70**, 90-92.

DOBSON, M.R. & WHITTINGTON, R.J. 1987. The geology of Cardigan Bay. *Proc. Geol. Ass.*, **98**, 331-353.

FITCHES, W.R. 1992. Chapter 4: Wales. *In* Treagus, J.E. (ed.) Caledonian Structures in Britain south of the Midland Valley. *Geological Conservation Review Series,* 3. Chapman & Hall, pp 97-104.

GARRARD, R.A. & DOBSON, M.R. 1977. The nature and maximum extent of glacial sediments off the west coast of Wales. *Marine Geology*, **16**, 31-33.

HAYNES, J.R. & DOBSON, M.R. 1969. Physiography, foraminifera and sedimentation in the Dovey Estuary (Wales). *Geological Journal*, **6**, 217-256.

JAMES, D.M.D. 1971. The Nant-y-Moch Formation, Plynlimon inlier, West Central Wales. *Jl. geol. Soc. Lond.*, **127**, 177-181.

JONES, O.T. 1909. The Hartfell-Valentian succession in the district around Plynlimon and Pont Erwyd (north Cardiganshire). *Qt. Jl. geol. Soc. Lond.*, **65**, 463-537.

JONES, O.T. & PUGH, W.J. 1916. The geology of the district round Machynlleth and the Llyfnant Valley. *Q. Jl. geol. Soc. Lond.*, **71**, 343-385.

JONES O.T. & PUGH, W.J. 1935. The geology of the districts around Machynlleth and Aberystwyth. *Proc. Geol. Ass.*, **46**, 247-300.

The Aberystwyth District

LOYDELL, D.K., 1991. The biostratigraphy and formational relationships of the upper Aeronian and lower Telychian (Llandovery, Silurian) formations of western mid-Wales. *Geol. J.*, **26**, 209-244.

LOYDELL, D.K., 1992-93. Upper Aeronian and lower Telychian (Llandovery) graptolites from western mid-Wales. *Palaeontographical Society Monograph*, 180 pp, 5 pls.

PHILLIPS, W.J. 1972. Hydraulic fracturing and mineralisation. *Jl. geol. Soc. Lond.*, **128**, 337-359.

WOOD, A. & SMITH, A.J. 1958. The sedimentation and sedimentary history of the Aberystwyth Grits (Upper Llandoverian). *Q. Jl. geol. Soc. Lond.*, **114**, 163-195.

The Aberystwyth District

APPENDIX 1. (M.R.D. & D.K.L.).

The general lithostratigraphy of the Upper Ordovician and Lower Silurian and Llandovery graptolite biozonation Additional information on the graptolite subzones of the A.G.F. and the B.M.F. is provided, and the Bouma turbidite cycle explained; post-depositional or diagenetic modifications to the turbidite and pelagic sediments are reviewed.

Llandovery Series	metres
Aberystwyth Grits Formation	240
Borth Mudstones Formation	350
Devil's Bridge Formation	300-600
Cwmsymlog Formation	0-140
Derwenlas Formation	20-100
Cwmere Formation	70-145
Ashgill Series	
Brynglas Formation	100-200
Drosgol Formation	370-40
Nantymoch Formation	290

The biozonation of the Llandovery, numbers refer to A.G.F. and B.M.F.

Stage	Biozone	Subzone
	insectus	
	lapworthi	
	spiralis	
	crenulata	
Telychian	*griestoniensis*	7. *caricus*
	crispus (c)	6. *proteus*
	turriculatus	5. *johnsonae*
		4. *utilis (a and b)*
		3. *renaudi*
		2. *gemmatus*
	guerichi	1. *runcinatus*
	halli	
	sedgwickii	
	convolutus	
Aeronian	*argenteus*	
	magnus	
	triangulatus	
	cyphus	
Rhuddanian	*acinaces*	
	atavus	
	acuminatus	

The Aberystwyth District

The lowest Telychian biozones (*guerichi-turriculatus*) have been divided into seven subzones. As the table above and Fig. 1 show, the A.G.F. and B.M.F. divisions include subzones 2, 3, 4a, 4b, 5, 6, 7, and c the *crispus* Biozone. The *crispus* Biozone occurs at the core of the AGF exposure in cliffs N of Llanrhystud (SN 534705).

Faunal details are contained in Loydell (1991, 1992, 1993) who showed that the diachroneity of the A.G.F. basal boundary is less than previously thought. The lowest graptolite horizons exposed in the New Quay area yield faunas of *gemmatus* Subzone 2 age whilst south of Borth (SN 630881) the oldest exposed are of *renaudi* Subzone 3 age; thus diachroneity approximates to one subzone. Each subzone perhaps, represents about 100,000 years.

Subzone (4a) occurs at Aberaeron, Constitution Hill Aberystwyth , Clarach S and Clarach N. At Aberaeron (SN 450626) where it consists of Tabce turbidite units with flutes or distinctly erosive bases and ripple cross-lamination. Tab parts of units are invariably thick, show grading and coarse-grained bases and complex amalgamations. Palaeocurrent directions towards the northeast are indicated both by flutes and ripple cross-lamination. Anoxic hemipelagites are preserved where thin-bedded units obtain. Indeed, there are several half-metre thick packets that consist of up to ten Tde units indicating episodes of abandonment. The sequence as a whole is considered to be a sandy lobe of the mid-fan zone.

Subzone 4 (undifferentiated) occurs at Llangwryfon where it consists of Tbcde turbidite units with plane-parallel bases characteristic of an outer sandy lobe environment. Subzone 4b occurs at Castle Rocks Aberystwyth, at Aberarth and at Craig Fawr Quarry, Penuwch.

Subzone 5 is found at Newbridge garage, Morial, Penparcau and Aberystwyth Harbour S. The southernmost confirmed exposure, located at Newbridge garage (SN 508594), has turbidite sequences more thinly bedded that at Craig Fawr Quarry Penuwch although the range of grain sizes are similar. The turbidites consist of Tabce units. Amalgamated beds were observed although turbidite units are commonly 25 to 30 cm thick. Ripple cross-lamination only occurs in the thicker turbidite units. Plane-parallel bases and the presence of granule grade material support a mid-fan lobe interpretation, although the absence of any consistency in bed thickness suggests proximity to a channel mouth. This subzone also occurs at Morial (SN 620795) and Aberystwyth Harbour S (SN 581809) where the sequences are dominated by Tcde units. Both ripple cross-laminations and convolute-laminations are present. At Moriah unit thickness and flute orientations compare closely with those at Aberystwyth S whilst at Penparcau (SN 590802) they are more varied, showing erosive bases, long wavelength ripple cross-lamination and northeastward palaeocurrent directions. In contrast with the underlying subzone the finer overall nature of the sequences, especially those

The Aberystwyth District

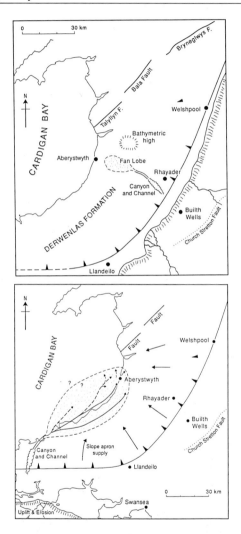

Figure 43: Sketches of fans in the Welsh Basin. The upper diagram shows the fan development during the Aeronian convolutus Biozone. During the preceding magnus - leptotheca biozones the fan lobe extended towards the south; in the succeeding sedgwickii-halli Biozones the lobe was directed towards the north. The lower diagram is a generalised sketch of the Aberystwyth Grits Formation fan during the early Telychian, mid - turrriculatus Biozone. Black triangles refer to the shelf edge.

The Aberystwyth District

at Newbridge, indicates a decline in detrial supply such that only outer-fan or distal lobe facies are present.

Subzone 6 has been recognised at Allt Wen and south to beyond Monk's Cave, but Subzone 7 has not been positively identified in the A.G.F. A higher biozone (c on Figure 1) occurs at Llanrhystud (SN 539697).

The classic fivefold subdivision of turbidite deposits (Tabcde), known as the Bouma cycle (Figure 44), allows the processes of sediment transport and deposition to be more easily appreciated. As the lower divisions (Tab) tend to accumulate at proximal or inner fan sites and the upper divisions at distal or outer fan sites it is rare for the whole cycle to be deposited together. Moreover, as there are several distinct sub-environments across a fan surface including channels, lobes and basin plains the application of the Bouma cycle may not always appear appropriate. Rapidly prograding sandy lobes consisting of amalgamated coarse-grained sandstones and conglomerates do not conform to the lower part of the Bouma cycle. Even so the model is valuable and will aid understanding of the patterns of sedimentation (Figure 44).

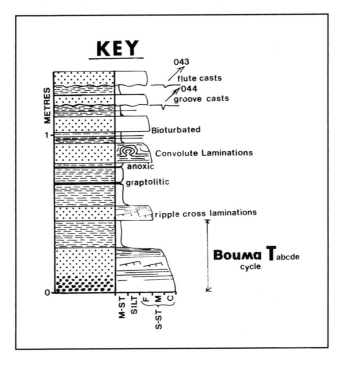

Figure 44: Key for the graphic logs of Aberystwyth Grits Formation.

The Aberystwyth District

Basin plain rhythms both in the A.G.F. and the B.M.F. consist of Bouma Tcde of Tde. Tc is a very fine grained sandstone or predominantly siltstone; Td is a medium grey silty mudstone; the interface between the two is distinct and non-gradational. Te is usually a grey structureless mudstone. In terms of bottom water oxicity at the time of interturbidite mud deposition, it is possible to distinguish 2 types: Type 1, pale and bioturbated muds; and Type 2, a dark grey pelagic mudstone, thinly laminated and graptolitic. With type 1 phosphatic concretions occur at the interface between Td and Te; with type 2 the interface is sharp without concretions. Phosphatic concretions formed from ionic migration across the interface between the oxygenated sediment and the turbidite mud below.

Of particular interest is the presence of pore-filling carbonate cement in the basal Tc layer. The cement is either ferroan dolomite or ankerite; the latter also forms large concretions. Initially the cement would have been calcite, but following deep burial iron, magnesium and aluminium were released during the transformation of smectite clays into illite. At high temperature the metal cations associate with the calcite cement to form ferroan dolomite and ankerite.

APPENDIX 2. Figures 45, 46, 47 & 48. (M.R.D.).

The sequence of events for the late Pleistocene to Holocene recorded in the sediments preserved in the Cardigan Bay area is given below.

9. Rapid sea-level rise with reworking of the till notably along the cliff line.

8. Extensive estuarine deposition in the Bay area between the sarnau 9,000 BP and widely developed coastal forests, between 6100 and 4200 years BP, that probably extended westwards along the sarnau ridges.

7. Formation of Head deposits; those along the cliff may include mobilised lateral morainic material (diagram 4, Figure 46).

6. Ice retreat, re-sedimentation of the Blue Till and extensive periglacial activity. Glacioisostatic rebound caused a marine regression phase. (diagram 3, Figure 46).

5. Mid-Devensian ice advance and deposition of the Welsh Blue Till, 26,000 to 13,000 BP. Glacioisostatic depression allowed marine waters into the South Irish Sea with glaciomarine sedimentation in the south (diagram 2, Figure 46).

4. Ice retreat and the reworking of the Yellow-Grey Till by fluvio-glacial and periglacial activity (diagram 1, Figure 46).

The Aberystwyth District

3. Deposition of the Yellow-Grey Till as a result of ice advance.

2. Fluvio-glacial reworking of this till following ice retreat, at the start of the Ipswichian interglacial, followed by a sea-level rise.

1. Deposition of the Welsh Brown Till during a pre-Ipswichian glacial phase, >70,000 BP.

A composite Quaternary stratigraphy and chronology for the margin of Cardigan Bay is shown in Figure 47; also included, for comparison, is a generalised sequence for the floor of Cardigan Bay. The coastal Quaternary sequences are varied and reflect the impact of cliff topography not only on the patterns of ice movement, but importantly on the slope-influenced processes that occurred periglacially. Two glacier complexes of Mid-Devensian age are known; an Irish Sea Ice complex that flowed southeast across Cardigan Bay reaching the coastal line south of Aberaeron; and a Welsh Ice complex which flowed out from the larger valleys into Cardigan Bay. Westward progress of the Welsh Ice was impeded by the Irish Sea Ice with the result that it turned southward and eventually stagnated. Thus the sarnau are both medial and terminal moraines of the Welsh Ice. It is also possible that during the brief movement south of the Welsh Ice lateral moraines developed along the cliff line.

The last glacial maximum occurred 18,000 BP and the maximum ice limit was south of the Carnsore Point to St David's Head line. Sea-level was lowered by at least 40 m. As a result of the overburden pressure of the ice sheet, glacioisostatic depression occurred throughout the region of Cardigan Bay and beyond. Thus, despite sea-level lowering the isostatic effects were such that a marine transgression took place during the early phase of ice retreat. Glaciomarine sedimentation is recorded at several sites along the Welsh coast, but most spectacularly on the coast near Cardigan at Mwnt (SN 193518). With the retreat of the ice, isostatic uplift continued until the post-glacial sea level minimum was reached 8,740 ± 110 years BP. The level was estimated to be 22 m below OD. Thus, extensive estuarine sequences recorded for Cardigan Bay are seen as regression deposits. The post-glacial eustatic sea-level rise followed this minimum and reached 5 m above OD. Over the last 5,000 years sea-level has fallen to its present position.

At Mwnt the glacigenic deposits, which are at least 30 m thick, infill a 100 m wide valley cut into Lower Palaeozoic mudstones and sandstones. From the road that serves the car park, access to the beach and the section of interest is by a well-maintained cliff path. In terms of ice source this area was dominated by Irish Sea Ice. From the beach level a sequence of 8 units, can be studied. The descriptions and interpretations for each unit are based principally on the work of M.E. Edwards of Trinity College, Carmarthen.

The Aberystwyth District

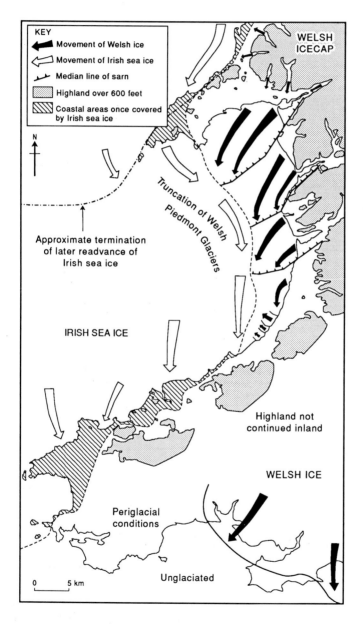

Figure 45: Ice masses and flow directions in Cardigan Bay.

The Aberystwyth District

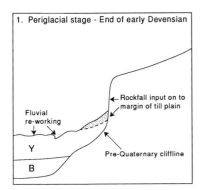

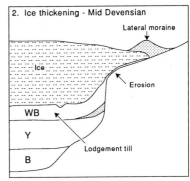

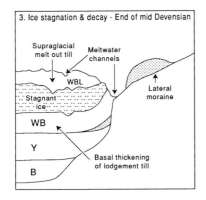

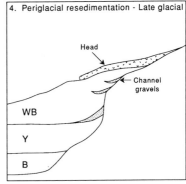

KEY

B   Brown Till (Pre-Ipswichian)   WBL   Blue Resedimented Till incorporating

Y   Yellow Till (Devensian)   lodgement and melt out tills plus

WB   Blue Lodgement Till (Devensian)   lateral moraine (Devensian)

Figure 46: Glacial and periglacial erosion and deposition along the Cardigan Bay coast modified after M. Gallop (1986) M.Sc. UWA.

The Aberystwyth District

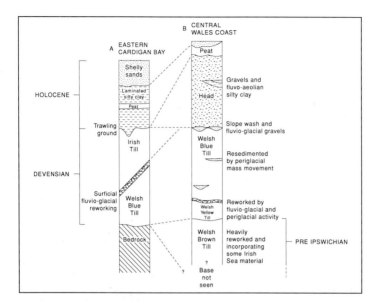

Figure 47: Generalised Pleistocene and Holocene stratigraphy for west Wales and Cardigan Bay, based In part on the work of Garrard and Dobson (1977) and M. Gallop (1986) M.Sc. UWA.

8. Sand, probably representing post-glacial aeolian deposition (variable thickness).

7. Gravel, probably an outwash deposit (2m).

6. Till, that could be a mass flow deposit associated with ice retreat (4 m).

5. Till, clast supported and massive (10 m).

4. Upper sands and gravels that reflect pulsed deposition close to the ice margin (25 m deformed as overfold).

3. Laminated sands and silts indicative of quiet water conditions with deposition coming from a suspension load (seen at north end only 2 m).

2. Lower sands and gravels with silt seen as fining upward cycles (2 m). This is an outwash deposit, probably localised in a meltwater channel.

1. Till, but only 1.5 m is preserved above beach level. Where seen it is massive and consolidated and whilst many of the included clasts are local, shell fragments and erratics typical of the Irish Sea Till are present.

The Aberystwyth District

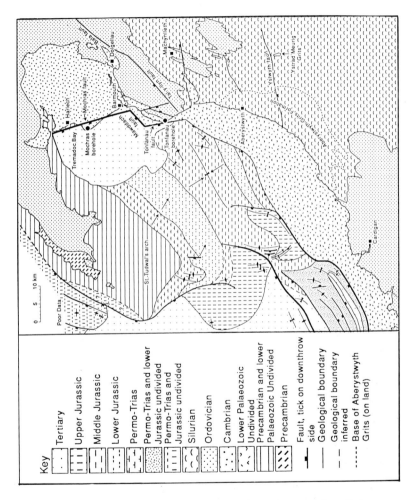

Figure 48: Sub-Pleistocene geology of the Cardigan Bay area from Dobson and Whittington (1987).

Unit 1 is recognised as a lodgement till; whereas units 2 to 7 accumulated during deglaciation in glaciomarine conditions predominantly from overflow plumes. Unit 4 slumped immediately following ice retreat.

The Aberystwyth District

GLOSSARY

ACID IGNEOUS ROCKS - Igneous rocks characterised by richness in the element silicon together with the elements sodium and potassium.

AGGLOMERATE - coarse volcanic pyroclastic material.

AMALGAMATED BEDS - This refers to turbidite beds where a layer, usually the graded Ta layer, is repeated several times to form a thick unit. Sometimes referred to as a multiple bed.

ANTICLINE - An arch-fold of a series of rocks.

ANKERITE - a calcium. magnesium, iron carbonate.

AXIS - The line along the outcrop about which the dip changes from one direction to the other. The 'axial plane' is seen as bisecting a fold structure.

BASIC IGNEOUS ROCKS - Igneous rocks relatively poor in the element silicon, and comparatively rich in the elements iron, magnesium and calcium.

BED - A layer of rock bounded above and below by distinct surfaces and composed of similar material. The thickness of a few centimetres to a metre or so is usually implied.

BOULDER CLAY - See Till.

BRACHIOPODS -One of the principal groups of shelled invertebrate marine animals. The shell has two valves, unequal in size.

BRECCIA - A hard rock containing an abundance of relatively large angular fragments mixed with finer material.

CIRQUE - A bowl-shaped hollow usually formed through the action of ice on a mountain side.

CLEAVAGE - In geology, a tectonic structure caused by general lateral pressure. It is well developed in fine-grained rocks. Note that cleavage may coincide with, or be oblique to bedding.

CLIMBING RIPPLES - With these ripples both the lee side and the stoss side are built up and preserved, thus causing the overall structure to increase in height or climb. The climbing eventually breaks down and the process starts again. For the structure to form, grains must be moving as bedload and settling out of suspension; that is why the structure is common in turbidite sequences.

The Aberystwyth District

CONCRETION - Spherical to irregular masses in sediments formed post-depositionally by precipitation from migrating pore fluids; see cone-in-cone below.

CONE-IN-CONE -Bands or concretions in argillaceous sedimentary rocks with an internal form as the name implies. Common in the distal facies of the Aberystwyth Grits Formation, and usually formed of ankerite.

CONFORMABLE - Beds are conformable when they lie one on another in a regular form.

CONGLOMERATE - An indurated sedimentary rock containing an abundance of grains larger than 2 mm.

CROSS-BEDDING - A sedimentary structure formed by the preservation of the lee slope of a migrating ripple form. It may be used as a current direction indicator hence the term current bedding.

DIACHRONOUS - This means across time, and is used to refer in a lithological sense to continuous beds, but which in fact represents the development of the same facies at different places at different times. This concept is best appreciated in the context of a transgression.

DOLERITE - A medium-grained basic igneous rock composed of calcic plagioclase feldspars and pryoxene and olivine. Also called a microgabbro.

FACIES - A rock type with particular characteristics; thus lithofacies. They usually indicate the environment of deposition under which they accumulated. Examples include sandstone facies, graptolite facies and shallow water facies.

FAULT - A surface of fracture along which there has been permanent displacement.

FLOW STRIPPING - A term used to describe the separation of the upper part of a turbidity flow from the lower part close to the bed. Separation is achieved most commonly at the bends in submarine channels.

GABBRO - A coarse-grained basic igneous rock.

GALENA - A heavy grey mineral with metallic lustre composed of lead sulphide.

GRADED BEDDING - Bedding in which there is a gradual upward transition of the grains from coarse to fine. Reverse grading refers to a transition from finer to coarser.

The Aberystwyth District

GRAPTOLITES - A group of extinct, marine, colonial organisms that were predominantly pelagic.

GREYWACKE - This is a lithological term used to describe a 'muddy' sandstone. In this context the 'muddy' term refers to the matrix of clay material that either was deposited at the same time as the sand size grains or in part formed post-depositionally from the breakdown of unstable grains like feldspars. High matrix sandstones are usually considered to have accumulated from a turbid flow rich in clay although the term greywacke is not restricted in its use to turbidites.

HEMIPELAGIC SEDIMENTS - These are of mixed detrital, including wind-borne material and volcanic debris, and organic origin, particularly biogenic skeletal material. In the Lower Palaeozoic sediments the principal component of hemipelagic layers is clay.

INTRAFORMATIONAL CONGLOMERATE - A sediment containing clasts coarser than 2 mm derived by erosion from within the same stratigraphical formation.

INLIER - An outcrop of older strata surrounded by younger strata.

LEAT - An open water course built to conduct water for mining operations.

NUÉE ARDENTE - dense incandescent volcanic ash-flow.

PERICLINE - A fold in which the dips are away from, or towards, a centre that is a dome or basinal structure. It is more commonly used for the dormal form.

SEQUENCE STACKING - This term may be applied to sedimentary rocks like sandstones that occur a series of massive units lying one on top of another.

SLICKENSIDES - A fault surface scratched and polished by the fault movement. Where the surface is mineralised then the term slickencrysts is applied to the mineral crystals.

SLOPE ENERGY - This is a function of gravity and is used when assessing the flow potential of turbidity currents from shallow water to deeper water.

STRIKE-SLIP - Faulting where the net relative movement is in the direction of strike of the fault plane.

TILL - This is a stiff impervious clay-rich deposit associated with glacial activity.

The Aberystwyth District

TRANSPRESSION - Compression usually oblique to a structural feature such as the line of subduction of a plate; this results in lateral movement usually on a strike-slip or transcurrent fault.

ZINC BLENDE - A dark mineral with resinous lustre, zinc sulphide. Also known as sphalerite.